GLOBAL SPIN

Probing the Globalization Debate

Where in the world are we going?

Randall White

DUNDURN PRESS
Toronto • Oxford

Copyright © Randall White, 1995

All rights reserved. No part of this publication may be reproduced, stored in a retrieval system, or transmitted in any form or by any means, electronic, mechanical, photocopying, recording, or otherwise (except brief passages for purposes of review), without the prior permission of Dundurn Press Limited. Permission to photocopy should be requested from the Canadian Reprography Collective.

Design by Andy Tong
Edited by Judith Turnbull
Printed and bound in Canada by Webcom

The publisher wishes to acknowledge the generous assistance and ongoing support of the **Canada Council**, the **Book Publishing Industry Development Program** of the **Department of Canadian Heritage**, the **Ontario Arts Council**, the **Ontario Publishing Centre** of the **Ministry of Citizenship, Culture and Recreation**, and the **Ontario Heritage Foundation**.

Care has been taken to trace the ownership of copyright material used in the text. The author and publisher welcome any information enabling them to rectify any reference or credit in subsequent editions.

J. Kirk Howard, Publisher

Canadian Cataloguing in Publication Data

White, Randall
    Global spin : probing the globalization debate

(Towards the new millennium series)
Includes bibliographical references and index.
ISBN 1-55002-237-7

1. International economic relations. 2. International relations.
3. Internationalism. I. Title. II. Series.

HF1359.W55 1995   337   C95-931841-0

Dundurn Press Limited
2181 Queen Street East
Suite 301
Toronto, Canada
M4E 1E5

Dundurn Distribution
73 Lime Walk
Headington, Oxford
England
0X3 7AD

Dundurn Press Limited
1823 Maryland Avenue
P.O. Box 1000
Niagara Falls, N.Y.
U.S.A. 14302-1000

Contents

List of Tables ... iv
Preface and Acknowledgments ... v

Prologue: Will "Globalization" Work? ... 1

1   Imperial Echoes: The Deepest Background ... 15
2   Technology and the Machine Civilization:
    What Everyone Really Wants ... 29
3   Twists and Turns:
    The New Economic Forces, 1970–1995 ... 42
4   The First Political Fallout:
    Free-Market Reform, the End of the Cold War,
    European Union, and the New Trade Agreements ... 58
5   Cultural Fallout: The High-Technological Mystique,
    New Migrations, and "Backlash" on Several Fronts ... 75
6   Tilting at Windmills: The Quest for
    Global Governance in the Twentieth Century ... 90
7   The Fate of the National State:
    Are We Serious about Democracy? ... 105

Epilogue: Some Parting Thoughts ... 121

Notes ... 129
Index ... 139

TABLES

1	The Most Populous Countries of the World, 1993	13
2	The World's Largest National Economies, 1993	14
3	The World's Most Widely Spoken Languages, 1993	28
4	The Seventy-five Largest Transnational Corporations, 1992	41
5	Share of Major Regions and Countries in World Production	57
6	Average Hourly Wages in the International Clothing Industry, 1992	57
7	The GATT Negotiating Rounds, 1947–1994	74
8	Cultural Diversity in North America, 1991	89
9	The Twenty Largest National Economies: GNP Per Capita, 1993	104
10	New Member States of the United Nations, 1990–1993	120

Preface and Acknowledgments

I was asked to write a brief but pointed introduction to the globalization debate for Dundurn Press's Towards the New Millennium series — a sequel of sorts to an earlier book I'd written on the historical background to the Canada-U.S. free-trade agreement of the late 1980s. And that is what I have done. Within a mildly argumentative analytic framework, this lean volume brings together an eclectic and, I hope, intriguing and even entertaining collage of relevant source materials for the convenience of readers who do not have the time to do the same thing themselves.

The book is marked by the plain facts that it has been published by a Canadian publisher and that its author resides in Canada. I have tried, however, to approach the subject from the standpoint of my status as an inhabitant of some larger universe. Personally, I am still impressed by Hannah Arendt's old-fashioned observation that "nobody can be a citizen of the world as he is the citizen of his country ... the very notion of one sovereign force ruling the whole earth ... is not only a forbidding nightmare of tyranny, it would be the end of all political life as we know it."[1] But I would certainly say that if there is anything unambiguously progressive about the globalizing trends of the late twentieth century, it lies in the extent to which these trends invite all of us to contemplate our shared humanity.

It is probably also worth noting that what practical experience I have with the subject comes from the bottom up rather than the top down. I first became more than intellectually interested in global political economy when I was working as a civil servant during the late 1970s. Just before an election some colleagues and I were asked to visit a number of recently troubled central Canadian manufacturing firms. I learned some new things talking with local corporate executives, including several managers of U.S. and other multinational branch plants. At some point later on I sensed — with something of the shock of a cold shower — the beginnings of dramatic change in the international economic system. I have continued to pursue this subject since then, and having left the civil service some fifteen years ago now, I have undertaken related assignments as an independent consultant. For reasons I cannot pretend to understand, I have always worked for those who are merely affected by globalizing trends, not those who are putting the trends in motion.

Essentially the same real-world path led to my earlier book on the Canada-U.S. free-trade agreement. I worked on this project during a period of combative domestic debate and under the pressure of various institutional deadlines. Although this book on globalization does not have the same formal structure (or the same deadlines) as the free-trade book, I have written it in a vaguely similar atmosphere – full of volatile controversy over such things as a draconian Canadian federal budget, the sudden devaluation of the Mexican peso, the collapse of the Barings PLC merchant bank in the United Kingdom, strong speculative pressure on the U.S. dollar, and the beginnings of a serious-enough trade skirmish between the United States and Japan.

The firmest conclusion I have drawn from my personal experience with such matters is that the best policy advice is "Always expect to be surprised." I am aware of the inadequacies of any undertaking to cover (as I attempt here) a great deal of ground in a short space – in a field where no amount of preparation can ever be enough. Speaking very briefly as a doctor of philosophy, however, I am confident that readers who take the steps prescribed in the following pages will at least be better prepared for the surprises that lie ahead.

I am indebted to Kirk Howard and Dundurn Press for the opportunity of unburdening myself on a subject that I have found increasingly fascinating for almost two decades. And as in other projects of this sort I owe ever-increasing debts to Jeanne MacDonald (who, among other things, once again conceived the title). I am also indebted to Judith Turnbull for her expert editorial skills and congenial advice on the original draft of the text, and to Andy Tong for his sure-footed work on the cover and layout of the book. For various other forms of aid and advice I am grateful to Frank Bunting, Peter Carruthers, Eileen Craig, Pat Dutil, Laszlo Gyongyossy, Tony Hawke, Dirk Lehman, Ian Low, David Montgomery, Nadine Stoikoff, Joseph White, and William White. I am grateful to the Ontario Arts Council for its support of the project's research budget as well.

In the notes at the back of the book, I have tried to indicate my debts to the eclectic assortment of technical and other literature on which my text is based. The sources for the various statistical tables that appear at the end of each chapter are marked on the tables themselves. It is worth stressing that all statistics are subject to a host of interpretive caveats: the simple ones I have included here are only meant to be suggestive, not to support any systematic theoretical arguments or major analytic claims.

Though it doesn't show up as often as it might in the notes, I should flag my own primary vantage point on the mainstream of the emerging global "I-way" by acknowledging my quite vast particular debt to *Business Week* magazine. I have been reading this U.S. publication more or less religiously since the late 1970s, and much of what appears in the following pages is in one way or another a reaction to its evolving interpretation of the growth of the world economy. While I frequently disagree with much of the magazine's political outlook, I think it does an admirable job of giving people like me something to disagree with.

In a related context it may seem that my text draws almost too much on the particular writing (or even, in an academic sense, the "political thought") of George Orwell. Some brief explanation is likely in order. I am not primarily interested here in the two grimly prophetic and rather untypical books for which "Orwell" is somewhat ironically best known. To me he remains an oddly prescient observer of Western public life, a person who profited from some unusual personal experiences in the emerging global village during the first half of the twentieth century. His sometimes almost cheerful and always deeply human essays and journalism still have strikingly relevant things to say about "the brute truth ... in world terms" – in a plain language that everyone can grasp. I think the globalization debate today could stand much more of his kind of voice.

In a far less adventurous way, I suspect that I have personally profited from the accident of residing in Toronto, a city whose present citizen body presents a cross-section of almost all the peoples currently extant in the world at large – a circumstance that at least ought to promote much well-informed global spinning within a conveniently compact chunk of the earth's geography. If I were to dedicate the book to anything, it would be to this diverse and still rather unformed[2] city, and to the great variety of quietly brooding hopes for a better future it harbours today.

R.W.
The Beaches, Toronto
July 1995

"This is, the headlines scream at us, the age of free markets and global capitalism. Every day, billions of dollars buzz across borders. Tons of goods traverse oceans. People pick up stakes and move clear across continents. Today, we are all citizens of the world."
Karen Pennar, *Business Week*, 1995

"... the overwhelming fact of our time is the rise of a global civilization, and if and when world order is achieved, the central problem may well be how to preserve the old variety of cultures within it. Whatever the event, this global civilization will be a blend of cultures which will no longer be dominated by Europeans."
John Bowle, *The Imperial Achievement:
The Rise and Transformation of the British Empire*, 1974

"... the cultures of different peoples do affect each other: in the world of the future it looks as if every part of the world would affect every other part."
T.S. Eliot, *Notes towards the Definition of Culture*, 1948

Prologue

Will "Globalization" Work?

"The world is too various; it can exist only in compartments in our minds."

V.S. Naipaul, 1982[1]

"Every once in a great while," the New York–based business writer Christopher Farrell recently intoned, "the established order is overthrown." On "the eve of the 21st century, the signs of monumental change are all around us." A "great transformation in world history is creating a new economic, social, and political order."[2]

Farrell is too elegant a writer to stoop all the way to the somewhat barbarous term "globalization" – the "favorite business buzzword for the 90s."[3] But this is a label others employ to characterize the monumental change he is talking about. And he does give a deft summary of what many seem to mean when they talk about globalization today:

> Communism's collapse and the embrace of freer markets by much of the developing world are driving huge increases in global commerce and international investment. The Information Revolution is forging strong links between nations, companies, and peoples. Improving education levels are creating a global middle class that shares "similar concepts of citizenship, similar ideas about economic progress, and a similar picture of human rights," says John Meyer, professor of sociology at Stanford University. Almost 150 years following the publication of the *Communist Manifesto*, and more than half a century after the rise of totalitarianism, the bourgeoisie has won.[4]

THE GLOBALIZATION DEBATE –
FROM THE BACK OF THE BUS

Similarly apocalyptic rhetoric currently comes in many high and low forms. In a recent morning's mail I received a special introductory issue of a U.S.

investment newsletter – "spawned in the Far East" and known as *Taipan*. It claims that "1995–2000" will be

> the most important years in human history …
>
> Many Christians believe this is the "end time." And the Babylonian astrologer Berossus taught that great conjunctions of the planets mark the end of great epochs of human civilization. In the final days of the second millennium, according to the ancient seer, the heavens will once again signal monumental changes.
>
> Taipan agrees, but for quite different reasons than planetary alignments or the Book of Revelations. We study long-term economic cycles and new technologies that are still in the lab stage. Our studies plainly tell us that gigantic changes are in the works – the biggest since 1492.[5]

It is one thing to sense historical turning points, however, and quite another to predict where the future actually lies. And it is probably a mistake to take any branch of the business press at its exact face value. All good business prose has a marketing edge. Its authors do not mean to be altogether serious about what they write.

The *Taipan* authors say you ought to buy their newsletter because they accurately predicted the collapse of the Soviet Union as early as 1980. But I would guess they know that many others regularly made the same prediction, in virtually every year since 1945. At the moment *Taipan* is making predictions about "new health companies whose amazing products might 'reverse the aging process.'" The phrase "reverse the aging process" has at least been put inside quotation marks, perhaps to guard against lawsuits.

Christopher Farrell's writing is much more scrupulous and sophisticated. There is no immediate product that he is trying to sell. There is some undeniable realism in what he says about "the embrace of freer markets by much of the developing world" and the "Information Revolution." Yet just how serious does he mean to be when he writes that "the bourgeoisie has won"? Is there any authentically serious sense in which such a thing as a "bourgeoisie" exists today even in the United States, let alone in such other populous global locations as Indonesia, Bangladesh, Nigeria, or Vietnam?

There can be no doubt, on the other hand, that the debate about globalization, to which both Christopher Farrell and the *Taipan* authors are making their own particular contributions, is becoming more and more serious in many parts of the world. This short book aspires to be one of many necessarily modest contributions to the same debate. I am not trying to sell anything either (beyond the book itself), and I do mean to be serious enough about everything I write.

My particular point of view, I believe, is that of at least one type of ordinary citizen of the planet – akin to what the nineteenth-century British political and economic writer Walter Bagehot once characterized as "the bald-headed man at the back of the bus." I should quickly add that I am only balding a little, on top, and I prefer streetcars and subways to any kind of bus. If I were to presume to rewrite Bagehot's phrase for the final days of the second millennium, I would of course pick an image less lamentably confined to the physique of a single gender.[6]

AN ANGLO-AMERICAN ILLUSION?

My point of departure in this volume is to argue that while some version of the globalizing trends Christopher Farrell alludes to are clearly now in motion, it is not at all clear just what they mean. It is equally unclear that, left to their own devices, these trends add up to any kind of "new economic, social, and political" *order*.

According to the cosmopolitan management guru Cyrus Freidheim, who over "almost three decades" has "lived on three continents and served clients in 20 countries across the world," the concept of a "global corporation" – the "model structure for a global market" – implies an organization that "develops and sources products with great efficiency worldwide." The organization "makes huge investments, which it amortizes across global markets." Its "executives are citizens of the world," and they "play no favorites." Freidheim believes that the concept points to "a great idea." But in the real world "it is largely a fiction."[7]

Even some business observers have lately been drawing highly sceptical conclusions from wisdom of this sort. According to another New York–based analyst, Debra Fleenor:

> Globalization is a set of ideas that do not necessarily work in our current business environment ... Globalization, like many trends in business, has created its own bandwagon. The bandwagon has become so widespread that those who are not on it are deemed provincial, and doomed to failure. This way of thinking is dangerous and misleading ... if the global path is without apparent destination, wise companies should consider choosing another route. In a wiser world, companies will not be following other companies down a dead-end street.[8]

Christopher Farrell himself is too wise an observer not to note the prospects of many potential dead-end streets among the signs of monumental change that are marking the eve of the twenty-first century. In many newly developing parts of the globalizing planet sweatshops and slums are commonplace, a Dickensian world of worker misery and raw social and political tensions. Fast growth in China and elsewhere creates dismaying environmental destruction ... Heightened international competition, along with rapid technological change, largely accounts for the 22.5% plunge in real hourly wages for high school dropouts from 1973 to 1993 in the U.S. ... In the industrial world, protests against the new competition are starting to get louder and take on a nasty edge ... Policymakers worldwide also worry that rising social and economic pressures in a competitive global economy will spark "culture wars." Hinduism vs. Islam. Confucian values vs. Western values. "The fault lines between civilizations will be the battle lines of the future," wrote Harvard University professor Samuel P. Huntington in an influential 1993 *Foreign Affairs* article.[9]

Farrell's own faith is that "given time, the triumph of the liberal ideas of the bourgeoisie, from free trade to democracy, coupled with the spread of technological innovations, should improve living standards throughout the world – bringing most people an opportunity for a better, richer life."[10] But from the standpoint of the bald-headed man at the back of the bus – in the increasingly advanced evolutionary stage that he or she has reached on the eve of the twenty-first century – it is easy enough to see Farrell's faith as an illusory and obsolete ideology, which leans too hard on its particular Anglo-American marketing edge.

Current globalizing trends are tied to an apparently inescapable economic logic. Yet almost half a century ago the Austrian-American economist Joseph Schumpeter explained that "there is an economic logic that has nothing specifically 'capitalist' about it."[11] It is not at all clear that "the triumph of the liberal ideas of the bourgeoisie" is what globalization means for the future. These ideas first came to light during the same late eighteenth-century era that saw the birth of the United States of America. Even if some globalizing trends did point in this direction, it is even less clear that the eighteenth-century liberal ideas of the Anglo-American bourgeoisie can successfully navigate the genuine challenges raised by the signs of monumental change that are all around us today.

AN ALTERNATIVE STRATEGY: THE USES OF HISTORY

To say that the present meaning of globalization is necessarily murky is not the same as saying that it is altogether unfathomable. The strongest impression that arises from any broad sampling of the recent talk and writing about the subject is of a kind of vast global confusion. But there are some at least less confused strategies for trying to make sense of current globalizing trends.

The key theme of this short book is that looking at the issues involved historically can bring fresh forms of realism to the wider debate. A recent United Nations technical report on the international economy has suggested one kind of rationale for this strategy:

> The steady growth of cross-border economic activity has produced considerable disagreement among economists ... [T]he growth and complexity of cross-border economic linkages are embedding the national organization of economic activity within a global system of processes and transactions. However, the extent, nature and implications of this change continue to be strongly contested – indeed, sceptics continue to see the current process of deeper integration as little more than the simple continuation of long-standing trends. Thus ... it is helpful to approach the globalization process from a longer-term perspective.[12]

Put another way, current globalizing trends are only the latest chapters in a story that already has some five centuries behind it. I find Christopher Farrell and even the *Taipan* authors convincing when they urge that the story has developed to a point where we are now at the edge of some new transformation in world history. But this transformation becomes less apocalyptic (or novel or "gigantic") when we ponder it in the context of its historical background. Somewhat paradoxically, perhaps, it also becomes more mysterious and open-ended.

You cannot even start to write "a history" of globalization in this sense in an introductory book like this one. My much more modest objective is to suggest a few crucial implications of putting late twentieth-century globalizing trends in a wider historical perspective. Living at the edge of a great transformation in world history may make the past seem less important at first. I am trying to suggest how, once you scratch the surface, it is impossible to be realistic about what such a transformation might involve without spending some time in the human laboratory of the world history that has already happened.

Using history to illuminate contemporary political and economic debate in this way differs methodologically from writing history from a rigorously disinterested standpoint. This book is most concerned with the history of the more recent past, because these are the parts of the story that have the most obvious relevance for us today. It is nonetheless important to keep the longest term in mind. Even for the narrowest purposes of illuminating the present, it is important to start the globalization story at its real and now quite remote beginning (as even the *Taipan* authors do, to their credit, when they refer to the "biggest" changes "since 1492").

There is another kind of methodological dimension to any form of historical writing, and it too can contribute to the realism of contemporary debate. History, as we have come to understand it, is a discipline that stresses the concrete over the abstract. Much of the globalization debate today, however, is conducted in highly abstract terms that too readily lend themselves to excess and exaggeration. In these circumstances plain description can sometimes take on unusual analytic power. There is a certain virtue, for instance, in setting an abstract concept like "global market" beside a concrete list of the most populous countries in the world, based on the most recent statistics available. Some will rightly object that, at the global economy's present stage of evolution, mere population numbers do not always add up to practical economic wight. They might prefer to consult a list of the world's largest national economies instead. Both types of list are included at the end of these introductory remarks (Tables 1 and 2). In either case the vastly different peoples and places involved suggest that, like Cyrus Freidheim's concept of a global corporation, in the real world the concept of a global market is still "largely a fiction" – and in some important senses is likely to remain this way well into the long-term future (or even beyond).

GLOBALIZATION AS AN IDEOLOGY

If globalization were strictly an economic phenomenon, longer- and shorter-term historical perspectives would only have consuming interest for economists. Part of what gives the globalization debate of today a much wider currency – and part of what makes our present circumstances fundamentally more dramatic than those of earlier chapters in the story of globalizing trends – is the extent to which economic developments have now begun to catalyze new forms of political and cultural ideology.

Christopher Farrell's New York–based writing about the great transformation in world history is one expression of this kind of ideology. But there are certainly others. On the opposite side of the Atlantic Ocean, Ron Meijer, from the Rotterdam School of Management in the Netherlands, has recently observed:

> Globalization is often not only seen as a cure-all for a range of management problems, but also functions for many as an ideology that fits in nicely with the Zeitgeist – the fall of the Wall, the disappearance of the other great ideologies, joint international policing efforts and increasing internationalization.[13]

There are intriguing (and, if you can put yourself in the right frame of mind, even amusing) ironies in the emergence of an ideology of this sort. Some picture it as an essentially right-wing phenomenon, closely linked with the multinational or transnational business community. In many respects Farrell's references to freer markets and the triumph of a global middle class fit this characterization comfortably. Yet in the end globalization as an ideology is more than a right-wing phenomenon.

In the first place, even those versions of the phenomenon that are essentially right-wing have taken on what used to be understood as essentially left-wing baggage, following the "fluid process of borrowing ideas from the ideological enemy ... familiar to all students of intellectual history."[14] In the nineteenth century it was the *Communist Manifesto* that ended with the ringing declaration "The proletarians have nothing to lose but their chains. They have a world to win. WORKING MEN OF ALL COUNTRIES UNITE!" The multinational organization with which the mature Karl Marx was affiliated was the International Working Men's Association. Even in the early twentieth century the *Internationale* – a French socialist "revolutionary hymn," composed in 1871 by Eugène Pottier – was the global communist anthem. In several respects Farrell's brand of late twentieth-century globalization ideology is a kind of Marxism turned inside out, with the bourgeoisie instead of the proletariat as the ultimate victors of the historical process.*

The democratic left also has its own globalizing heritage in this sense. Various expressions of this heritage play a part in the globalization debate today. One frequently cited passage in the recent globalization literature comes from *The Work of Nations* by Robert Reich, currently best known as the beleaguered Bill Clinton's beleaguered secretary of labour:

> We are living through a transformation that will rearrange the politics and economics of the coming century ... As almost every factor of production – money, technology, factories, and equipment – moves effortlessly across borders, the very idea of an American economy is becoming meaningless, as are the notions of an American corporation, American capital, American products, and American technology. A similar transformation is affecting every other nation.[15]

---

* One could talk as well about the inspiration Marx derived from his fellow German philosopher Hegel in this connection, and about the gloss on Hegel in Francis Fukuyama's recent book, *The End of History* (personally I do not at all think that history is about to end).

In the English-speaking world at large, even the contentious late twentieth-century gospel of political correctness can be understood as a species of globalization ideology. The surprising social power that the gospel began to acquire during the age of Margaret Thatcher and Ronald Reagan was partly a tribute exacted by one branch of the left from one branch of the right – a kind of cultural interest paid on some useful borrowing from the ideological enemy. It "is of the highest importance," George Orwell wrote towards the end of the Second World War, "that Socialists should have no truck with colour prejudice." People in Asia and Africa "will be looking at *us*, the Labour movement, to see whether our talk about democracy, self-determination, racial equality and what not has any truth in it."[16] In Christopher Farrell's much more recent formulation, late twentieth-century "capitalism is triumphant because it is multicultural."[17]

Here as elsewhere my argument is that it would be wrong to jump to conclusions. What is most interesting about globalization ideology today is not that it is inherently right-wing or left-wing (the current cases of China and India would seem to suggest that it can be either, or perhaps sometimes neither), but rather that it reflects how globalizing trends are now raising much more than narrow economic issues. A young man with old family ties in Asia put this point forcefully during a recent local public affairs television show I happened to catch: "You can't have globalization of economics," he urged, "without globalization of culture."

IN THE NORTH OF NORTH AMERICA

One of the more provocatively titled contributions to the recent globalization literature is Richard O'Brien's *Global Financial Integration: The End of Geography*.[18] Yet the still somewhat more recent United Nations technical report I cited earlier has concluded that, provocative titles aside, "geography still matters." Robert Reich's kind of argument, that transnational corporations "have, in effect, become de-nationalized ... is only a partial interpretation of the real world."[19] The UN authors cite still other passages from the literature to support this contention:

> However great the global reach of their operations, the national firm does, psychologically and sociologically, "belong" to its home base. In the last resort its directors will always heed the wishes and commands of the government which has issued their passports and those of their families.[20]

> Differences in national economic structures, values, cultures, institutions, and histories contribute profoundly to competitive success.

The role of the home nation seems to be as strong or stronger than ever. While globalization of competition might appear to make the nation less important, instead it seems to make it more so.[21]

A broad sampling of the literature suggests as well that geography continues to have a parallel impact on contributions to the globalization debate itself. Even the urbane populism of the bald-headed man at the back of the bus varies from one place to another. In evaluating any particular contribution to the debate, readers ought to consider the concrete geographical circumstances from which it has sprung.

I spend most of my time in (to borrow some language from the incomparable Jane Jacobs) the largest city region in the most northern country in North America – Toronto, Canada. Though Canada has, for the moment, one of the world's ten largest national economies,* it is no kind of big player on the global political and economic scene. Its vast and rugged geographic territory is actually larger than that of the United States, but in the middle of the 1990s its population was less than 30 million people – a little smaller than Argentina's and slightly larger than Algeria's or Tanzania's. It is the home country for only a few large multinational or transnational corporations.[22] An artifact of the earlier histories of first the French and then the British empires, Canada is now widely perceived outside the country as a mere political, economic, and cultural satellite of the U.S.A.

In the past few decades, however, Canada has been periodically buffeted by instructive globalizing trends. It has lived through two fractious domestic debates on apparently path-breaking new international trade agreements. It has embarked on a tortuous constitutional debate – sparked by the latest incarnations of long-standing nationalist aspirations in the predominantly French-speaking province of Quebec, and in several respects shaped and even prompted by global forces. Early in 1995 the Canadian federal government introduced a quite draconian budget, hoping to convince the international financial community that the country is utterly determined to control its public debt.

Even in the age of the global village, national geographic realities like these still have meaning for people who feel a part of them. As a matter of principle, I think, any book that tries to put late twentieth-century globalizing trends in a wider historical perspective ought to be written from an ostensibly global viewpoint. This is what I have at least tried to do here. Yet it is also part of my argument that, in practice, a globalization author's par-

---

* According to the "standard measure" of gross national product calculated by the World Bank. See the table at the end of these introductory remarks.

ticular national geography is bound to intrude on his or her text, from time to time and in various quiet ways.

More than anything else, my own geographic circumstances dramatize the point that globalization is not just something that concerns what Farrell calls "a wealthy international elite of cosmopolitan professionals comfortable working for companies headquartered in New York, Tokyo, or Buenos Aires."[23] If it were, it would not be at all as interesting (or as new and "monumental") as it is. What makes the subject so serious – and so unavoidable – is that it increasingly affects everyone, even in the home countries where most of us still spend most of our time.

OVERVIEW: SEVEN HISTORICAL STEPS TO THE FUTURE

The pages that follow present seven short sketches of the wider historical background to the globalizing trends that affect everyone today – starting with events that occurred as long as some 500 years ago, but stressing the much more recent past:

The Heritage of European Imperialism

The first sketch discusses the origins of the late twentieth-century global adventure in the imperial expansion of Europe that began during the late fifteenth century. What we are now calling globalization is both more and less than a final fling of the discredited old imperialism. But it does remain a kind of progeny of the historic "European sea-borne Empires."[24]

The Technological Heritage

In several senses technology is and has been the great driving force behind globalizing trends. We immediately think of the late twentieth-century microelectronics revolution in this context. Yet the most striking technological feature of globalizing trends today has older roots. What George Orwell was already calling "the machine civilisation" in the 1930s[25] – the new material universe that takes such things as automobiles, electrical household appliances, indoor plumbing, and telephones for granted – has finally begun to spread beyond the so-called first world of Western Europe, North America, and Japan.

The New Economic Forces

During the decades immediately following the Second World War, the dominant political energy behind the quest to diffuse the machine civilization around the globe lay on the left. New economic forces that settled in during the 1970s, 1980s, and earlier 1990s have shifted the politics of modernization to the right. It is ironic (in more than one sense) that some key parts of the so-called third or developing world have finally begun to develop under the apparent auspices of capitalism rather than socialism.

Some Early Political Implications
By the middle of the 1990s the new economic forces had generated a first wave of political and institutional realignment. This wave takes in the spread of various versions of the political ideology of free-market reform, the end of the Cold War and the collapse of the Soviet Union, the rise of a new kind of economically and perhaps even politically integrated Europe, regional trade agreements in the Americas and Asia, and, at the end of the long Uruguay Round of the General Agreement on Tariffs and Trade, the creation of the World Trade Organization.

Cultural Implications
The new economic forces have prompted a variety of increasingly notable cultural reactions. Some of these reactions focus on the new technologies of the microelectronics revolution as the key economic agents of cultural change. Various new migrations of people are probably more important, and they raise ambiguous prospects for at least limited new forms of global culture. The new economic forces have prompted cultural backlash as well.

The Global Governance Revival
Cultural backlash has helped revive interest in an older quest for innovations in international governance. There is a clear need, many would argue, to manage the accelerated globalizing trends that the new economic forces have set in motion. The present United Nations and an assortment of related organizations can claim some modest success. The global governance movement has obvious continuing importance, but it remains highly fragile and underdeveloped.

Democracy and the National State
The accelerated globalizing trends spawned by the new economic forces of the 1970s, 1980s, and earlier 1990s have at least begun to erode some historic options of the nation-state. But its fundamental monopoly of legitimate force remains intact. The spread of the national state throughout the world has itself been part of the globalization process, and the great majority of UN member states in the middle of the 1990s are quite recent creations. Above all else, the national state remains the only viable framework for the democratic political system. My argument here is that, in the end, we will discover

that the national state also remains the most important political framework for coping with many of the new problems that the dramatically accelerated globalizing trends of the late twentieth century are setting before us.

* * *

By the end of the last of these seven sketches readers ought to be in a better position to draw their own conclusions about just what globalization is and whether it will work. I do not think many decisive answers are possible right now. But the answers that are possible do strike me as more engagingly mysterious (if also more tough and challenging) than much of the current debate seems to suggest. The book ends with an epilogue that summarizes the main thrust of what I think myself. In a general way, I suspect that if some of those who talk the loudest about globalization today ever do live long enough to discover what it really means, they will be quite surprised.

Table 1
The Most Populous Countries of the World, 1993
(Population, 000s)

Country	Population
China	1,175,359
India	900,543
United States	258,063
Indonesia	187,151
Brazil	156,406
Russian Federation	148,537
Japan	124,845
Pakistan	122,829
Bangladesh	116,702
Nigeria	104,893
Mexico	86,712
Germany	80,769
Vietnam	70,881
Philippines	65,775
Iran	61,422
Turkey	59,461
Thailand	58,824
United Kingdom	58,040
Italy	57,840
France	57,650
Egypt	55,745
Ethiopia	53,297
Ukraine	52,141
Myanmar ("Burma")	44,704
South Korea	44,056
Zaire	40,997
South Africa	40,677
Spain	39,125
Poland	38,446
Colombia	35,682
Argentina	33,483
Canada	27,815
Sudan	27,255
Algeria	26,882
Tanzania	26,743

Source: The World Bank Atlas 1995

Table 2
The World's Largest National Economies, 1993
(Gross National Product, Millions of U.S.$)

United States	6,387,686
Japan	3,926,668
Germany	1,902,995
France	1,289,235
Italy	1,134,980
United Kingdom	1,042,700
China	581,109
Canada	574,884
Spain	533,986
Brazil	471,978
Russian Federation	348,413
South Korea	338,062
Mexico	324,951
Netherlands	316,404
Australia	309,967
India	262,810
Switzerland	254,066
Argentina	244,013
Sweden	216,294
Belgium	213,435
Austria	183,530
Denmark	137,610
Indonesia	136,991
Iran (1992 data)	130,910
Saudi Arabia (1992 data)	126,355
Turkey	126,330
Thailand	120,235
South Africa	118,057
Norway	113,527
Hong Kong	104,731
Ukraine	99,677
Finland	96,220
Poland	87,315
Portugal	77,749
Greece	76,698

Source: The World Bank Atlas 1994, 1995.

CHAPTER ONE

IMPERIAL ECHOES

THE DEEPEST BACKGROUND

"There are no limits to our Naval Power, but those by which the Creator has confined the Globe."

W. Watts, 1757[1]

The earliest beginnings of what is called the globalization process in the late twentieth century can be traced as far back as the start of the sea-borne imperial expansion of Europe, in what the Western Christian calendar calls the fifteenth century. Nevertheless, Christopher Farrell and the *Taipan* authors are not just straining for effect when they talk about the current "great transformation in world history" or the biggest changes since 1492. Even to use such expressions as fifteenth or twentieth century only makes sense in terms of the Christian religion, which is adhered to by only one-third of the world's present population at most. Intellectually, it is now all too obvious that an authentic conception of world history ought to employ a more universal global calendar, perhaps rooted in what is said to be the appearance of our most immediate human ancestors some 40,000 years ago.

Similarly, from what we do know about the subject at this point it seems clear enough that different regions and cultures have played prominent roles at different strategic moments in the planet's human evolution. According to the late 1970s *Times Atlas of World History*, which can credibly claim to be at least "world-wide in conception," it "was almost certainly from some part" of a lineage in Africa "that the first recognisably human creature ... finally evolved." Agriculture began in "the Near Eastern region of the Old World." The first regional civilizations arose in "the fertile alluvial basins of the major rivers which water the otherwise arid plains of southern Asia."[2]

It is an equally plain fact that the first ocean-going travellers who pioneered our present comprehensive grasp of the world's geography set out from the Atlantic coasts of Europe, and not from some other part of the globe. But this does not imply any unique virtue in the regional civilization of "Christendom," which took shape on the European continent after the fall of the Roman empire. Europe was only catching up, as it were, with the earlier strategic contributions to world history that Asia and Africa had already made.

THE PORTUGUESE PIONEERS

The comparatively limited and cut-up nature of the land in Western Europe may say something about why people from such places as Portugal, Spain, France, the Netherlands, and England built and manned the first vessels capable of regular long-distance journeys across forbidding global seas. It also ought to be instructive that the particular group of people who began the global adventure came from a country that would later be viewed as a "small, rather poor, culturally backward nation, perched on the south-west coast of Europe."[3]

In today's globalization literature Portugal is often treated as an emerging rather than a developed market, in the same class as countries like India, Mexico, Thailand, and Zimbabwe.[4] Five hundred years ago it was a dynamic centre of innovative international trade and exploration. The pioneering late twentieth-century historian Immanuel Wallerstein, author of *The Modern World-System*, has devoted some half-dozen pages to explaining why it was Portugal that first expanded "overseas and not other European countries." (He also used almost twice as much space to discuss why it was in Europe, and not in the then comparably populous China, that globalizing overseas expansion first began.)[5]

For our purposes here it is enough to note that in 1487, after several decades of Portuguese naval contact along the west coast of Africa, Bartholomew Diaz doubled the Cape of Good Hope and stumbled upon a sea route into the Indian Ocean. By 1498 Vasco da Gama had reached India. In the wake of these exploratory voyages, quite ruthless Portuguese traders, in well-armed carracks and galleons, established fortified outposts at Sofala (1505) and Moçambique (1507), on the east African coast. In 1510 they wrested Goa on the west coast of India from the Sultan of Bijapur. A year later they captured Malacca, on the southwestern coast of the Malay Peninsula. In 1515 they conquered Ormuz on the Persian Gulf.

Starting in 1539, Portuguese settlers began to colonize the coast of Brazil in the new world of the Americas. Around 1557 Portuguese traders established an outpost in the obscure Chinese fishing village of Macao. By 1570 there was a similar Portuguese trading outpost in the Japanese fishing village of Nagasaki. By the late sixteenth century Portugal commanded a vast seaborne trading network that stretched from Brazil in the far west to Japan in the far east:

Among the important products of this far-flung empire were the gold of Guinea (Elmina), of south-east Africa (Monomotapa) and of Sumatra (Kampar); the sugar of Madeira, São Tomé, and Brazil; pepper from Malabar and Indonesia; mace and nutmegs from Banda; cloves from Ternate, Tidore and Ambonia; cinnamon from Ceylon; gold, silks and porcelain from China; silver from Japan; horses from Persia and Arabia; cotton textiles from Cambay (Gujarat) and Coromandel.[6]

Being first is not easy. The perhaps too-far-flung Portuguese empire began to atrophy very quickly. Early on it had turned down the overtures of the Genoese navigator Christopher Columbus, who then "discovered" the Americas in 1492 for Portugal's larger and more populous neighbour, Spain. By 1521 Ferdinand Magellan had laid a Spanish claim to the Philippine Islands.

In 1575 Portuguese forces were defeated by the Sultan Baab at Ternate (in present-day Indonesia). By this point the expansive Ottoman Turks were challenging Portuguese supremacy in the Persian Gulf as well. By the end of the sixteenth century there were early stirrings among new European imperial rivals, in the Netherlands and in France and England. In 1641 the Portuguese lost Malacca to the Dutch (who would then lose it to the British in 1824).

As early as the middle of the seventeenth century – when the colonial settlements of New England and New France were just starting to take root in North America – the Portuguese empire had shrunk to a pale imitation of its former self:

> The epic days of plunder gave way to a settled and inefficient exploitation that grew ever more inert as decade followed decade and century century ... Deepening conservatism, deepening reluctance to adjust to a changing world became the hallmark of the Portuguese ... Rigid, orthodox, decaying, mouldering like an antique ruin in the tropical heat, the Portuguese empire slept on.[7]

The history of the world nonetheless has its own logic. The first seaborne empire of Europe would also be the last to give in to the decolonizing forces that have helped turn the old imperialism into the new globalization in our own time. The government of India that achieved the country's independence from the British empire in 1947 finally had to seize Goa from Portugal by force in 1961. Portugal's African colonies in Angola and Mozambique did not become independent until 1975.

OLD AND NEW WORLDS

The deepest continuing legacy of the Portuguese empire is probably the language of Brazil – the fifth most populous country and tenth-largest national economy in the world today. Brazil became independent from Portugal in 1822, but Portuguese remains its official language. More people in the world now speak Portuguese than either German or French.

The example of Brazil underlines a fundamental distinction between European expansion in the old and new worlds. In the old worlds of Asia and Africa the successive imperialisms of Portugal, Spain, the Netherlands, France, and England were largely managerial enterprises, driven by ruthless quests for wealth and prestige. There was little enduring European mass settlement, and the underlying cultures of these European colonies remained fundamentally Asian and African. But in the new world of the Americas – and in the later cases of Australia and New Zealand – new European colonial societies, built around mass migrations, largely supplanted the earlier indigenous cultures (for which there is still no satisfactory general name).

Europeans, of course, were not the only newcomers in the Americas. It is all too true that European expansion in the new world was brutally linked with the black African slave trade. The ultimate revenge of the descendants of slavery has been that much of what is most innovative and interesting about American culture today has deep African roots. There was also some Asian migration to the Western Hemisphere before the twentieth century. On current historical assumptions, the indigenous "Indian" peoples of the Americas had themselves originally migrated from Asia (though many of their present-day descendants dispute this claim). Yet the new European colonial societies that arose in the new world during the sixteenth, seventeenth, and eighteenth centuries inevitably leaned hardest on models in Europe. The languages that prevail throughout the Americas today are European languages.

Clearly, within the new world not all the European models were the same, but there is a particularly provocative distinction between the English- and French-speaking new societies in the north and the Spanish- and Portuguese-speaking societies of the south. There had been more elaborate indigenous cultures in the warmer new world regions than in the north, and descendants of these cultures remain unusually numerous in several countries of present-day Latin America; yet, apparently for inherently European reasons, the colonies of Portugal and Spain never became altogether "modern." Even in today's globalization literature, countries like Mexico, Brazil, and Argentina (like Portugal itself) are still "emerging markets."

Within the old world there is a distinction between those parts of Asia and Africa that eventually became European colonies, of one sort or another, and those that did not. China in the seventeenth and eighteenth centuries did not have time for barbarians from Europe. It was too busy with the transition from the Ming to the Qing (or Manchu) dynasty, its already rapidly increasing population, and its own imperial expansion in East Asia. Later on all the major European powers acquired Chinese commercial interests, but China never became a part of any European empire in the same sense as India became the brightest jewel in the British monarch's crown.

Europe's early expansion in the old world was far from overwhelming, and the great and inescapable high tide of European imperialism in Asia and Africa did not arrive until the late nineteenth century. Throughout the sixteenth, seventeenth, and eighteenth centuries there were many parts of the earth's surface that no one in Europe or most other places even knew about, except for the people who lived in them. Sea-borne Western Europeans gradually stumbled on the comprehensive knowledge of world geography we now take for granted. European commercial interests established footholds in various far-flung places, but Western Europe did not at all dominate the globe, as it would for a brief period later on.

In the late seventeenth century representatives of the English East India Company landed in Japan, which had already reacted against its earlier experience with Christian traders from Portugal. Japanese officials "wished the English merchants a pleasant voyage and long lives, but refused to treat with ships wearing any sort of cross."[8]

THE SEVEN YEARS' WAR AND THE BRITISH EMPIRE

In all its historic phases the imperial expansion of Europe had "no central agency which acted in terms of ... long-range objectives"[9] or tried to resolve conflicts among rival Europeans. By the early eighteenth century the Spanish, Dutch, French, and English competitors of the already somnolent Portuguese were seriously getting in each other's way.

In 1756 the resulting struggles boiled over into the Seven Years' War. According to the U.S. historian Samuel Eliot Morison, this protracted conflict "should really have been called the First World War." Earlier fighting between French and English and their respective "Indian allies" in North America merged dramatically with war in continental Europe,

> where it was France, Austria, Sweden, and a few small German states against Britain and Prussia. England supported Prussia with money and engaged in naval warfare against France (and later Spain) in the Atlantic, the Mediterranean, the Caribbean, and the Indian Ocean. There was warfare on the continent of India between French under Dupleix and English under Clive and their respective native allies;

hostilities even reached the Philippines, where an English fleet captured Manila ... [H]ostilities were waged over as large a portion of the globe as in 1914–1918.[10]

One resounding outcome of the Seven Years' War was the triumph of the upstart British imperial enterprise – "the last and greatest of the European sea-borne Empires."[11] After several generations of taking a back seat to France (and Spain) in terms of global reach, the half-century-old United Kingdom of England and Scotland enjoyed an *annus mirabilis* in 1759. The English writer Horace Walpole "complained that the church bells were worn threadbare with ringing for victories" around at least several different parts of the world.[12]

In 1776, however, the British Thirteen Colonies in America wrote their Declaration of Independence. In the same year the Scottish economist Adam Smith published the first edition of his book on *The Wealth of Nations* – the new free-market gospel of "the liberal ideas" of the Anglo-American bourgeoisie. A few currents in the politics of the American War of Independence also spilled over into the subsequent French Revolution. And it was a Frenchman, Alexis de Tocqueville, who wrote the still classic account of the early United States, *Democracy in America*, in the 1830s.

By the time the first volume of de Tocqueville's book had appeared, most of the more southerly colonies of Latin America had followed the U.S. independence precedent, helped along by the impact of the Napoleonic Wars in Portugal and Spain. The British empire retained a strategic position in North America through its mid-eighteenth-century "conquest" of the earlier French Canada. Britain, France, and the Netherlands would directly control an assortment of colonial outposts in the Caribbean well into the twentieth century, but by the end of the first quarter of the nineteenth century the European economic and cultural presence in the new world had lost the most important of its original political moorings.

In the old worlds of Asia and Africa, on the other hand, the late eighteenth and nineteenth centuries were marked by increasingly sweeping bursts of fresh European expansion. "Vast new zones" were brought into a European-dominated "world economy."[13] And this economy increasingly did dominate large parts of the globe. The old ruthlessness that the Portuguese had first brought to the process of global expansion took on ruthless new forms. The Opium War of 1839–42 opened up eventually fatal cracks even in the celestial empire of China, which "until the 17th century ... had remained superior to the West in many ways."[14]

The now aging Spanish empire had "grown arthritic." The "Portuguese possessed the rigidity of a corpse."[15] But the Dutch consolidated their position in the Indonesian archipelago. The French expanded into Southeast Asia and North Africa. On a more grandiose scale altogether, the overseas enterprises of what became the United Kingdom of England, Scotland, and Ireland on 1 January 1801 blossomed into "the empire on which the sun never sets" and "the greatest empire since Rome." In the wake of the Seven Years' War and the American War of Independence,

> the British retained and augmented their paramountcy in India and extended it to Burma, consolidating the massive strategic base for their power in the East and Australasia. They regained control of the Atlantic, the Caribbean and the western Mediterranean, and, after the Napoleonic Wars, extended it by the annexation of Malta and the control of the Ionian isles to the Levant. They took over the Cape Colony and Ceylon from the Dutch, and Mauritius from the French; under the Regency they established themselves at Singapore, and in 1842 at Hong Kong. The second war with the United States of 1812–1814 fended off the American attempts on Canada, and a strategic base on Vancouver Island could be developed on the north Pacific; while the convict settlement made in Australia in 1782 began to take on strategic importance both for the south Pacific and New Zealand. The British emerged ... to become the greatest world power of the nineteenth century with an overwhelming naval and industrial supremacy.[16]

RUSSIA, AMERICA, AND JAPAN

Every historical epoch "contains a great deal of the last epoch"[17] – and of the next one as well. Much of what we have known in the later twentieth century has its own imperial echoes from earlier eras. As vast as the British empire became, it never commanded or even dominated anything at all like the entire globe. Even at the height of its grandeur, new upstart rivals were groping towards new forms of global reach.

As early as the sixteenth century the East European state of Russia had embarked on a dramatic "land-borne" imperial expansion into Asia. In 1533 Russia extended no farther east than the Ural Mountains – traditionally regarded as the boundary between the Asian and European continents. Over the next dozen decades "the lucrative fur trade ... tempted enterprising Russians deeper and deeper into Siberia, until the Pacific coast was reached (1649) and the Russian hold established over the whole of northern Asia."[18]

During the nineteenth century the Russian empire expanded again, into the territories (*khanates*) populated by Islamic nomads southeast of the Ural Mountains and east of the Caspian Sea. When the Union of Soviet Socialist

Republics was established, on the heels of the Russian Revolution of 1917, it inherited both the particular international socialist ideology forged by the German Karl Marx (who spent most of his adult life in London, England) and the expansionary conquests and impulses of the earlier Russian empire. This earlier Russian imperialism would become one historical key to the break-up of the Soviet Union in the early 1990s.

The land-borne Russian expansionary experience was also an unacknowledged precedent for the late eighteenth- and nineteenth-century westward expansion of the new United States of America. Down to the end of the American Civil War in 1865, the politically independent United States remained something of an economic and financial colony of its former British imperial masters. The American banking dynasty of the House of Morgan began in 1835, when the Baltimore merchant George Peabody sailed to London to renegotiate the defaulted debt of the state of Maryland with British bankers. To this day the state of Mississippi "remains in unashamed default" on debts contracted with British banks in the first half of the nineteenth century.[19]

With striking speed, however, after the Civil War the United States created its own autonomous and increasingly dynamic economic power base, and began to rival its former British masters in an expanding world economy. "Before 1914 the most renowned international currency was the British pound, and the financial capital city of the world was London; by 1918 the dollar replaced the pound, and New York, London."[20] The side of U.S. political culture that looked to the more radical Declaration of Independence in 1776 was anti-imperialist; the side that looked to the more conservative federal constitution of 1789 was ready to assume the burden of European imperialism, even before Europe itself began to falter. The upshot was that "American imperialism ... has been made plausible and attractive in part by the insistence that it is not imperialistic."[21]

Yet even the land-borne westward expansion of the United States had clear imperial overtones. Apart from ruthlessly ravaging the Mohicans, the Cherokee, the Sioux, and the Apache, the U.S. acquired Texas and California, both of which had originally belonged to Mexico. And, though ostensibly intended to protect the new political independence of Latin America, the Monroe Doctrine of 1823 nonetheless presumed a kind of U.S. imperial paternalism for all of the new world. By the end of the nineteenth century the federal government at Washington had begun to pick up pieces of the collapsing Spanish empire in the Caribbean and the Pacific.

One especially pregnant act of nineteenth-century American imperialism took place as early as March 1854, when Commodore Matthew Perry landed in Japan. Bearing gifts of a miniature railroad and telegraph, Perry managed to cajole the Japanese into signing the Treaty of Kanagawa, which opened the ports of Shimoda and Hakodate for trade with U.S. ships. This marked the beginning of the end for the long regime of the impressively isolationist Tokugawa shogunate,* established in 1603 to shield the Japanese from the destructive edges of the early globalization process launched by the Portuguese.

The shogunate had banned Christian missionaries from Japan after 1612, forbidden the Japanese to travel abroad, and limited foreign contacts inside Japan to the Chinese, the Koreans, and the Dutch (who inherited the old sole Portuguese trading post at Nagasaki). The Tokugawa period was highly repressive – "somehow dark and menacing. Too many gifted people were squelched."[22] But by the time it had ended "Japan was prosperous, well governed, had a high standard of literacy, and was far better prepared than China to meet the challenge of Western expansion."[23]

With the ironically named "Meiji Restoration" of 1867, Japan rapidly began to transform itself into Asia's first self-sustaining modernized economy, capable of joining the expanding European-dominated world economy on something close to its own terms. With equal rapidity it also fashioned an early Asian counter-imperialism of its own. In 1895 it emerged triumphant from the Sino-Japanese War and annexed the Chinese island of Taiwan. To the shock of the great powers of Europe, it defeated the restless Russian empire at the Battle of Mukden in 1905. By 1933 it had established the protectorate of Manchuko on the Chinese mainland. During the Second World War it overran much of the British, French, and Dutch empires in south and Southeast Asia.

THE HIGHEST STAGE OF CAPITALISM

Just as the new Japan of the Meiji Restoration was taking shape, the seaborne imperial expansion of Europe reached its great and inescapable high tide. According to the recent United Nations technical report cited earlier, the "period 1870–1913 has, in particular, been seen as" a high point in the historic growth of the global economy.[24]

---

* Broadly, a shogunate was a system of rule by the commander-in-chief of the Japanese army (as opposed to the emperor), and there have been various examples in Japanese history. Tokugawa Ieyasu was made shogun by the imperial court in 1603, though the shogunate he founded is sometimes dated from 1600, when he effectively consolidated his military power. The Tokugawa shogunate endured until 1867 (sometimes dated 1868), when, as Japanese tradition has it, the emperor was "restored."

According to Christopher Farrell's version of the same events, the "period from 1870 to 1913," like the late twentieth-century period we are living through today,

> was a time of vast international capital flows. In 1913 the share of foreign securities traded in London was 59% of all traded securities; and by 1914, the stock value of foreign direct investment had reached an estimated $14 billion, or one-third of world investment. Some 36 million people left Europe; two-thirds of them emigrated to the U.S. and an even larger number of Chinese and Indians went to Burma, Indonesia and elsewhere. Trade soared, technological innovation flourished, and economic growth surged.[25]

In 1916 Vladimir Ilyich Lenin gave a classic polemical account of the same period in world history, in a short book entitled *Imperialism, The Highest Stage of Capitalism*. Late twentieth-century technical reports on the international economy by United Nations officials are bureaucratic documents, which necessarily evade all forms of political controversy, but some of Lenin's earlier critical perspectives can be extracted from between the lines of the more recent historical writing by UN authors.

The new and vast international capital flows followed "two rather different globalization paths in the period prior to the First World War." On the first path, investment in new industrial manufacturing activity "was concentrated in Europe and North America" – that is, in the home countries of the most established and most European-oriented rising imperial powers. On the second path, investment in the primary resources that served as grist for the industrial manufacturing mills was a more genuinely global process.[26]

Investment "in the primary sector was also strongly complemented by investments in transportation and trade." But the gains from this process "accrued largely to the capital exporting (commodity-importing) countries" in the European heartland. Some of the largest recipients of the new global investment "(such as China and India) experienced a period of 'de-industrialization.'" In many cases the second path "was reinforced by colonial governance structures."[27]

The importance of colonial governance structures helped prompt the political "partition of Africa" between 1880 and 1913. Belgium, Italy, and Germany (the bristling new land-borne power of central or "middle" Europe) had been left out of the earlier scramble for colonies overseas, partly because they were themselves new political creations of the nineteenth century. They now joined in on the ultimate wave of imperial expansion.

As late as 1879 the interior of Africa was "almost unknown to the

European powers; an intricate kaleidoscope of tribal kingdoms and traditional hunting grounds."²⁸ By 1913 the entire continent had been divided up among the Belgians, the British, the French, the Germans, the Italians, the Portuguese, and the Spanish – except for Liberia, Ethiopia, and the somewhat special case of the "Anglo-Egyptian Sudan."

By this point political, economic, and cultural stresses and strains inside and outside the European continent had set the stage for the official First World War, which began in the summer of 1914. Political and military leaders initially imagined that the fighting would be wrapped up in a matter of months. But it carried on for almost four and a half years, wreaking havoc and destruction in many parts of the globe. The end of the conflict set another stage for the gradual but seminal decline in European power and influence that would mark the twentieth century.

DECOLONIZATION IN THE GLOBAL VILLAGE

The late nineteenth century was also a time of rising resistance to the seaborne empires of Europe in some of the most strategic non-European regions of the globalizing planet. "The 'new imperialism,' beginning with the French occupation of Tunis in 1881 and the British occupation of Egypt in 1882, unleashed an anti-colonial reaction throughout Asia and Africa, the extent, intensity and significance of which have rarely been fully appreciated."²⁹

The Indian National Congress, which would evolve into the governing political party of today's India, was formed in 1885. Just after the end of the First World War, in 1919, the British Parliament passed the Government of India Act, which introduced to India

> a system of dual government or "Dyarchy" by which Indians were given representation in elected assemblies as well as having higher posts in the civil service open to them. Important areas of government and financial control were still reserved to the occupying power, yet it was considered a great step forward in India, the beginning of a process of deliberate education towards eventual self-rule – perhaps by the end of the century.³⁰

By the end of the Second World War it was clear that "education towards eventual self-rule" had already taken place, in about half the scheduled time. In 1947 India became an autonomous British dominion. In 1950 it chose to declare itself an independent republic.

Over the next three decades the colonial governance structures of all the old global empires of Europe were almost completely dismantled, in one way or another. "In our time, direct colonialism has largely ended." Imperialism has become "a word and an idea today so controversial, so fraught with all sorts of questions, doubts, polemics, and ideological premises as nearly to resist use altogether."[31]

And yet many different old imperial legacies persist in today's global village. Transnational corporations are key implementing institutions of the late twentieth-century globalization process, and according to the United Nations, of the more than 37,000 such institutions operating in the world today, more than 33,000 (and all of the "top 100," ranked by foreign assets) still have their home countries in Western Europe, North America, or Japan.[32]

The Arab-American literary critic Edward Said has recently urged that the lingering histories of the sea-borne empires of Europe have bequeathed amorphous, anxious, and agonized cultural legacies to contemporary globalizing trends as well:

> Hardly any North American, African, European, Latin American, Indian, Caribbean, Australian individual – the list is very long – who is alive today has not been touched by the empires of the past ... This pattern of dominions or possessions laid the groundwork for what is in effect now a fully global world. Electronic communications, the global extent of trade, of availability of resources, of travel, of information about weather patterns and ecological change have joined together even the most distant corners of the world. This set of patterns, I believe, was first established and made possible by the modern empires.[33]

Already the great transformation in world history that looms ahead is forcing us (whoever we may be) to face up to still unexamined implications of this old imperial groundwork, in ways we have only begun to think about. There are many new voices that wish to be heard:

> In our wish to make ourselves heard, we tend very often to forget that the world is a crowded place, and that if everyone were to insist on the radical purity or priority of one's own voice, all we would have would be the awful din of unending strife, and a bloody political mess, the true horror of which is beginning to be perceptible here and there in the resurgence of racist politics in Europe, the cacophony of debates over political correctness and identity politics in the United States, and ... the intolerance of religious prejudice and illusionary promises of Bismarckian despotism à la Saddam Hussein and his numerous Arab ... counterparts.[34]

Grappling with all this successfully, it seems to me, is finally bound to take the imminent worldwide transformation some considerable distance beyond the eighteenth-century liberal ideas of the Anglo-American bourgeoisie. Even if we avoid the sharpest forms of cultural conflict that Samuel Huntington has predicted, the old European imperial origins of today's globalizing trends will continue to germinate many troublesome adventures.

Strong and sustained growth in a genuinely global economy could no doubt do a lot to contain the truest horrors that these adventures portend. But, over the mid- to longer term, one prerequisite for this kind of growth would seem to be to face up to and take practical account of the as yet unexamined implications of the old imperial groundwork.

Politically, culturally, and economically, the globalization process already has a history of some 500 years behind it. The simplest message of this history, I think, is that globalization is a problem that begs solutions. It is not a solution itself.

Table 3
The World's Most Widely Spoken Languages, 1993
(Millions of Speakers Worldwide)

Mandarin (China)	952
English	470
Hindi (India)	418
Spanish	381
Russian	288
Arabic	219
Bengali (India)	196
Portuguese	182
Malay-Indonesian	155
Japanese	126
French	124
German	121
Urdu (Pakistan, India)	100
Punjabi (India, Pakistan)	94
Korean	75
Telegu (India)	73
Marathi (India)	70
Tamil (India, Sri Lanka)	69
Cantonese (China, Hong Kong)	66
Wu (China)	65
Javanese (Indonesia)	64
Vietnamese	64
Italian	63
Turkish	59
Tagalog (Philippines)	53
Min (China, Malaysia)	50
Thai	50
Swahili (East Africa)	48
Ukrainian	47
Kannada (India)	44
Polish	44
Gujarati (India, Pakistan)	41
Hausa (West Africa)	38
Malayalam (India)	35
Hakka (China)	34

Source: S. Culbert, University of Washington, Seattle.

CHAPTER TWO

Technology and the Machine Civilization

What Everyone Really Wants

"... it seems somehow a pity that the very concept of homesickness is presently going to be abolished by the machine civilisation which makes one part of the world indistinguishable from another."

George Orwell, 1936[1]

Military battles are not always as significant as those who fight them tend to believe. One deeper explanation of the British empire's great leap ahead of its European imperial rivals in the late eighteenth and nineteenth centuries is that the British industrial revolution, customarily viewed as having begun in earnest around 1780, was the first industrial revolution in history.[2] (Something related could be said as well about the later great leap forward of the U.S.A. – the historic British empire's most resounding legacy to the world at large.)

It can also be argued, on the other hand, that the industrial revolution took place first in Britain because, thanks to the British army and navy, by the late eighteenth century the British empire had gained command of the largest overseas markets: "Behind our Industrial Revolution there lies this concentration on the colonial and 'underdeveloped' markets overseas, the successful battle to deny them to anyone else ... Our industrial economy grew out of our commerce, and especially our commerce with the underdeveloped world."[3]

INDUSTRY, EMPIRE, AND THE MASS OF THE PEOPLE

Trying to solve the chicken-and-egg problem in the industry and empire relationship cannot be a direct part of our purposes here. But it is worth noting that the relationship itself gradually became a part of the internal left-wing critique of British society in the twentieth century. Just before the start of the Second World War George Orwell wrote:

What we always forget is that the overwhelming bulk of the British proletariat does not live in Britain, but in Asia and Africa ... [T]he per capita annual income in England is something over £80, and in India about £7. It is quite common for an Indian coolie's leg to be thinner than the average Englishman's arm ... This is the system which we all live on and which we denounce when there seems to be no danger of its being altered.[4]

One crucial point about the late twentieth-century globalization process is that this system is at last starting to be altered. The alteration is not happening in the way earlier left-wing critics envisioned it would (and it is still rather limited), but it is happening nonetheless. Another of Orwell's prescient judgments is more obviously apt today than when he wrote it. "On occasion," he argued in 1948, the British "left-wing parties" were

ready to admit that the British workers had benefited, to some extent, by the looting of Asia and Africa, but they always allowed it to appear that we could give up our loot and yet in some way contrive to remain prosperous. Quite largely, indeed, the workers were won over to Socialism by being told that they were exploited, whereas the brute truth was that, in world terms, they were exploiters. Now, to all appearances, the point has been reached when the working-class living standard *cannot* be maintained, let alone raised. Even if we squeeze the rich out of existence, the mass of the people must either consume less or produce more.[5]

Such bleak arguments draw stark attention to another crucial point. The only way out of this particular Orwellian dilemma that anyone has ever thought of is through the power of technological development. This power reached soaring new heights in the industrial revolution, first in Britain, where the revolution began, and then in other parts of Western Europe, in North America, and in Japan.

It is no doubt in some senses true that the growth of industry has historically depended on various kinds of empire. But it is also true that the growth of empire has depended on industry. This two-way relationship is especially important for Edward Said's "fully global world" of the present, "made possible by the modern empires." Orwell himself grasped that only technology and the "machine civilisation" can finally enable the mass of the people to produce more. To a great extent the progressive potential of the long march towards the global village depends upon a faith in "the social possibilities of machinery" – a sense that human-beings "are only as good as their technical development allows them to be" and that "without a high level of mechanical development human equality is not possible."⁶

ARABIC NUMERALS: A PRELUDE

Because the industrial revolution began in Britain, it is sometimes imagined that technology is an essentially European or Western creation. Yet one of the most significant technological developments in the broadest sweep of world history was the invention of agriculture. And the world had agriculture long before the culture of Western Christendom even started to take shape.

Improvements in the science of overseas navigation were also prerequisites for the globalization process initiated by the Portuguese in the late fifteenth century – some 300 years before the industrial revolution. However, the technological key to Portugal's and Spain's leadership in early globalizing trends was their earlier long incubation in (or proximity to) the vast Moorish empire of the new Islamic faith, which had spread like a desert storm over the Mediterranean and Near Eastern regions of the globe after the prophet Mohammed's triumphal return to Mecca in A.D. 630.

By A.D. 730 the Islamic empire "reached from Spain and Southern France to the borders of China and India." It would display "spectacular strength and grace, while Europe lapsed in the Dark Ages." It may have been its sheer size

> that made it a kind of bazaar of knowledge ... It may have been a quality in Islam as a religion, which, though it strove to convert people, did not despise their knowledge ... the science of the conquered nations was gathered with a kleptomaniac zest ... the knowledge of Greece and of the east was treasured, absorbed and diversified.

One particular Greek invention that "Islam elaborated and spread was the astrolabe." It measured "the elevation of the sun or a star" and, coupled with assorted maps, "also carried out an elaborate scheme of computations that could determine latitude, sunrise and sunset."⁷

It was Islamic Arab astrolabes and maps that carried the early Portuguese pathfinders into the Indian Ocean. In the fourteenth and fifteenth centuries much of the scientific knowledge that Christian Europe knew about had been passed on by Arab hands. This was particularly true of the ancient Greek knowledge that Europe would later come to think of as its own, forgetting the "Asiatic influence which flows all through Greek culture and which we commonly overlook." When the English poet Geoffrey Chaucer "wrote a primer to teach his son how to use the astrolabe" in 1391, "he copied it from an Arab astronomer of the eighth century."⁸

Another invention crucial to later European technological development also came through Arab hands, from a still more distant and unambiguously Asian source. During the historic incubation of modern Europe, "the spread of mathematics from India to Baghdad and the Moorish universities of Spain implied the gradual substitution of Arabic for Roman numerals and an enormous increase in the efficiency of calculation."[9] The science of "writing numbers" was the "most important single innovation that the eager, inquisitive, and tolerant Arab scholars brought from afar."[10]

Though the science did not start to take hold in Europe until the late thirteenth century, the Arabs had brought from India, in about A.D. 750, what the English language still calls Arabic numerals, and along with them, the modern decimal system.[11]

> [The] debt of the Western world to India in this respect cannot be over-estimated. Most of the great discoveries and inventions of which Europe is so proud would have been impossible without a developed system of mathematics, and this in turn would have been impossible if Europe had been shackled by the unwieldy system of Roman numerals.[12]

These ancient Indian mathematical traditions no doubt have something to do with late twentieth-century India's emerging status as a key world centre for the design of computer chips and software.

THE FIRST AND SECOND INDUSTRIAL REVOLUTIONS

Francis Bacon (1561–1626) and especially Isaac Newton (1642–1727) made decisive contributions to the early development of mathematics and science in England. But the first industrial revolution, which took off in the 1780s, draws at least as much attention to "the crude, trial-and-error, hit-or-miss nature of technological progress."[13]

The crux of the revolution was of course the use of machines in the production of goods that had formerly been produced largely by human (and animal) labour, and this led to a dramatic increase in the quantity (and, in some senses, the quality) of goods available. The capacity to use machines in this way had been developing in England since the earlier part of the eighteenth century. By the 1780s, in the wake of the American War of Independence, the capacity had reached a seminal fruition.

The first revolutionary industrial goods were cotton textiles. Their story includes such figures as the "unscrupulous operator" Richard Arkwright (1731–92), who "unlike most real inventors of the period ... became very rich."[14] The first great industrial machine was the steam engine (patented by its real inventor, the Scot James Watt, in 1769, and patented again in a more practical version in 1781).

The first industrial revolution, which "began in England in the eighteenth century, spread therefrom in unequal fashion to the countries of Continental Europe and a few areas overseas" in the nineteenth century. Wherever it went, it introduced a new kind of material culture, based on the particular industries that lay at its heart – "textiles, iron and steel, heavy chemicals, steam engineering, railway transport."[15]

In a number of respects, the new material culture of this first revolution still had more in common with the world of the seventeenth and eighteenth centuries than with the developed world of today. During the late nineteenth century, however, "the rise of new industries based on spectacular advances in chemical and electrical science and on a new, mobile source of power – the internal combustion engine" created a fresh "cluster of innovations that is often designated as the second industrial revolution."[16]

Especially after the First World War, this second industrial revolution spawned the spectacularly revolutionary material culture that George Orwell would refer to as the "machine civilisation" in the 1930s. It was dominated by the automobile, labour-saving electrical appliances, a galaxy of mass-produced consumer goods, motion pictures, phonograph records, and the radio. It progressed most rapidly in North America, where traditional institutional and geographic barriers to change were weaker than in Europe (or in Japan). And, above all in the United States, it brought the benefits of the new industrial technology to the mass of the population in compelling and unprecedented ways.

One difference between the first and second industrial revolutions was the increasing importance in the second of science, in the sense of "rigorously systematized knowledge within a consistently formulated theoretical framework." If "one had to choose any fifteen-year period in history on the basis of scientific breakthroughs that took place, it would be difficult to find one that exceeded 1859–74."[17] And this period of theoretical progress helped pave the way for the practical innovations of the second industrial revolution. Even in the later nineteenth century, however, the prolific American inventor Thomas Edison had never finished primary school. He had more in common with his one-time employee Henry Ford (who did finish primary school, but then went straight to work) than with the university-educated author of the 1873 scientific classic *Electricity and Magnetism*, James Clerk Maxwell.

Perhaps the largest difference between the first and second great waves of technological change in the new industrial era lay in the depth of their impact on society at large. The high tradition of European architecture, art, and music in the nineteenth century still kept a faith of sorts with the preceding several hundred years, but by the early twentieth century there were drastic new directions (which – alas, some would say – have now found their way into the popular culture of the global village).

CRITICS OF THE FIRST AND SECOND WAVES

Most twentieth-century analysts, whatever their partisan political persuasion, would agree that the early industrial revolution bred gross new forms of social injustice. It "tended, especially in its early stages, to widen the gap between rich and poor and sharpen the cleavage between employer and employed."[18] It divided "producers" into "two classes. The first gives its labour and possesses nothing else ... The second commands capital, owns the factories, the raw materials, the machinery, and reaps the profits."[19]

A great deal has been written about capitalism and socialism in this context, and the subject breeds complications that now seem less interesting than they did fifty or even twenty-five years ago. It is nonetheless worth noting that the industrial revolution did not create what came to be called capitalism in the middle of the nineteenth century. According to Karl Marx ("one of the first to try to work out an explicit model of the capitalist process"),[20] the "evolution of modern capitalism began at the time of the Renaissance and with the discovery of the New World,"[21] during the early rise of the European sea-borne empires that launched the globalization process.

On these assumptions, already well-developed capitalist forms of economic organization – created by the European bourgeoisie, which was taking shape at about the same time as the sea-borne empires – were prerequisites for the effective mobilization of the new technology of the industrial revolution.* In its more sophisticated manifestations (and Marx's writing is one of them), the socialism that arose in Western Europe during the nineteenth century stressed the importance of capitalism in mobilizing the new technology. But socialism also offered the first great critique of the European industrial revolution brought about by capitalist means. Socialism embraced what it saw as a new instrument for ushering in an age of human freedom and equality, but it urged that the potential of technology could only be realized

---

* It is worth noting in this context that, like the sea-borne empires, printing by means of moveable type first appeared in Europe during the fifteenth century. So-called block prints in Europe were "possibly introduced from China during the Mongolian supremacy." European "block books began to appear as early as 1409." The earlier "spread of Buddhism and writing and printing in China" had been "accompanied by an expansion of the paper industry and by its migration to the West through the Mohammedans." (Harold Innis, *Empire and Communications* [Toronto: University of Toronto Press, 1950, 1972], 139–40.)

for everyone when government, acting in the interests of the producers who gave their labour and possessed nothing else ("the proletariat"), seized command of the new industrial society from the capitalists ("the bourgeoisie" – in its highest forms at least), who owned the factories and the machinery, and reaped the profits for themselves.

For better or worse, history has been hard on the socialist critique. Even democratic governments in countries that had already industrialized by capitalist means were deeply embedded in capitalist economic interests. It proved stupendously difficult for socialism to revolutionize an ongoing capitalist industrial society. In practice, what became the democratic socialist movement finally found itself concentrating on strengthening labour interests through collective bargaining over wage rates, and on using government to create what amounted to capitalist social welfare states. Rather ironically, the attempt to implement socialism in its most Marxist or revolutionary communist form took place in countries that had never had a capitalist industrial revolution. Socialism in this sense became an effort to create an alternative, non-capitalist model of industrialization, through the agency of government or "the state." And, as the ultimate failure of the alternative model that was attempted between 1917 and 1989 in Russia now seems to confirm, Karl Marx and his nineteenth-century colleagues were right when they stressed the importance of capitalism in the initial mobilization of the new industrial technology.

Socialism in virtually any of its senses was not critical of technology or against the industrial revolution. Socialists believed, as Orwell put it, that "without a high level of mechanical development human equality is not possible." Before but especially in the wake of the second industrial wave and the revolutionary machine civilization of the twentieth century, however, a much more direct critique of the new technology gained momentum. It did (and still does to some degree) challenge the industrial revolution itself.

This more direct critique has taken various forms and has bred its own share of complications. During the early nineteenth century the legendary Luddites of the English East Midlands smashed their machines in a random protest against the rising early industrial society. With much more sophistication, as recently as the 1970s "the broad discussion initiated by the Club of Rome on the limits to industrial growth" systematically cast doubt on the assumption that "social progress must be borne on the wings of technology."[22]

Since the end of the Second World War the most sophisticated and telling criticisms of the industrial revolution have come from the ecological arguments of the environmental movement, which began to acquire serious political weight in the 1960s. The hypothesis that mindless technological expansion is now upsetting a wide array of self-regulating systems in the world of nature has both a direct and broad popular appeal, as well as the same scientific patina that lends so much prestige to technology (or much more superficially, to "bourgeois economics").

At the same time, in its most rational forms the environmental critique seeks merely to modify rather than to reject the industrial revolution. As in other contexts, Orwell was a prescient observer. In the 1940s he anticipated current concerns with "soil erosion and squandering of the world's fuel resources." He urged that we ought to "use the products of science and industrialism eclectically, applying always the same test: does this make me more human or less human?" But he accepted that "all sensitive people are revolted by industrialism and its products, and yet are aware that the conquest of poverty and the emancipation of the working class demand not less industrialisation, but more and more." And he grasped one key message of today's globalization process: even for socialists the "fearful poverty of Asia and Africa" implies that "the problem for the world as a whole is not how to distribute such wealth as exists but how to increase production, without which economic equality merely means common misery."[23]

THE THIRD (AND FOURTH?) REVOLUTIONS TODAY

It would have been easier for almost everyone if the progress of the industrial revolution had not been somehow entangled with the expansion of the European sea-borne empires, in such a way that one part of the world became rich while other parts stayed poor. It would have been easier as well if the capitalist forms of economic organization that so successfully mobilized the early new industrial technology had not also done so much to widen the gap between rich and poor, even within those parts of the world that became rich.

At the very least, it would have been easier if the industrial revolution had stood still long enough after creating its flawed technological blessings for the flaws to be removed by high-minded acts of human will. By the time the second revolutionary wave had created the new machine civilization, even George Orwell was agreeing that "the manual workers throughout most of the world are probably better off, in a physical sense" than they had been before. In a few places they were "unquestionably better off."[24]

But the history of the world has never been so easy in any of these respects. In one crucial sense the industrial revolution did not just happen once or even twice in the past. It began a process with many waves, and the waves have kept on coming, without leaving the planet much time to catch its breath. By the 1960s there were "those who say, for example, that we are already in the midst of the third industrial revolution, that of automation, air transport, and atomic power" (and analysts with less austere personal habits would give television a prominent place on the same list).²⁵

Only a generation later, in the 1990s, while there is much less consensus about the future of atomic power, more than a few would claim that already the third industrial revolution has, with quite dizzying speed, given way to a dramatic fourth wave of change – one "based upon the microelectronics revolution and, in particular, what has come to be seen as the major new generic technology: information technology." This latest information age "defines a new techno-economic paradigm since the introduction of information technologies has 'such pervasive effects on the economy as a whole that they change the style of production and management throughout the system.'"²⁶

As seasoned viewers of North American television commercials can attest, each revolutionary development does tend to become less revolutionary as the number of such things increases. But there can be no doubt at all that the increasing speed of technological change since the end of the Second World War has dramatically accelerated the globalization process that began with the Portuguese mariners in the fifteenth century:

> The cumulative improvements in transportation technology have continued to reduce the time and cost of moving materials, products and people across space ... [T]he evolution of the jet aircraft from turbo-prop to jet propulsion dramatically shrank global distances so that, for example, New York is now closer to Tokyo in terms of travel time than it was to Chicago in the latter half of the last century.²⁷

Even allowing for all its tiresome hype, by the middle of the 1990s it is clear enough that today's information age is bringing powerful new tools to historic globalizing impulses. The information age blends "communications technology, which is concerned with the transmission of information, and computer technology, which is concerned with the processing of information." The "new telecommunication technologies are establishing truly global electronic highways," and the costs of using these highways are rapidly falling. In "the late 1960s the annual cost of an Intelsat telephone circuit was more than $60,000; twenty years later it was $9,000 and in 1994 was under $5,000." Ultimately,

> it is the combination of the two technologies – exemplified by satellite and optical fibre technologies, facsimile machines, computer-aided design and manufacturing systems – that is most significant for the processes of internationalization and globalization of economic activities. Although reinforcing the international production

of a number of activities that have traditionally contained a large information or knowledge component (such as financial activities), these technologies ... are increasing the knowledge component of traditional manufacturing activities, enabling firms to redeploy their production ... in a more geographically dispersed fashion.[28]

For those among us who live in the so-called developed or first world, there is nonetheless a crucial sense in which the industrial revolution is an event that did happen largely in the past. From the consumption as opposed to the production and management side of the global economy, the new tools of the information age are essentially only talented handmaidens in the increasingly wider geographic diffusion of the second-wave machine civilization.

Even with all its continuing problems of social injustice, environmental degradation, aesthetic torpor, and moral ennui, the machine civilization – which takes such things as automobiles, electrical household appliances, indoor plumbing, modern medicine, motion pictures, and telephones for granted – has already brought the great mass of the population in some parts of the world a life so transparently better than anything that went before as to render all but the most theological debate on the subject superfluous. It is hardly surprising that this is what the great mass of the population in the rest of the world wants as well. And, at the bottom of everything else, how it is going to get it is what the late twentieth-century globalization debate is all about.

TECHNOLOGY AND THE TRANSNATIONAL CORPORATION

In the late 1960s the left-wing British economic historian Eric Hobsbawm stressed one fundamental difference between the difficulty in spreading the technological blessings of the twentieth-century machine civilization across the globe and the difficulty in starting the first industrial revolution in Britain. Some 200 years ago the "technology of cotton manufacture" and "that of most of the rest of the changes which collectively made up the 'Industrial Revolution'" were "fairly simple." They "required little scientific knowledge or technical skill beyond the scope of a practical mechanic of the early eighteenth century."

On the other hand, in the "'emerging' nation of today which sets about its own industrial revolution," the "most elementary steps forward ... assume a command of science and technology which is centuries removed from the skills familiar to more than a tiny fraction of the population until yesterday." The "most characteristic kinds of modern production" are "of a size and complexity which put them beyond the experience of most of the small class of local businessmen who may have hitherto emerged, and require a quantity of initial capital investment far beyond their independent powers of capital accumulation."29

A quarter of a century later it is even more complex and costly to put the new technologies of the microelectronics revolution into motion. Even in the developed world the substantial minority of mechanically minded consumers who once happily fixed and maintained their own automobiles have become increasingly baffled by the new technologies under the hood. The commercial repair expert who fixes my television set just seems to replace large boxes of complicated electronic parts that he (or she) understands no better than I do.

Whatever else it may or may not have done, the continuing industrial revolution, in its increasing technological sophistication, has created some very large, complex, and inevitably powerful new human organizations. This points to the rise of the fabled multinational or, as the United Nations prefers, "transnational"* corporations – Royal Dutch Shell, Exxon, IBM, General Motors, Hitachi, Matsushita Electric, Nestlé, Ford, Alcatel Alsthom, and General Electric (to take only the ten largest in the world today).30 According to a sympathetic analyst of the 1970s, they have "come to be seen as the embodiment of almost anything disconcerting about modern industrial society."31 According to a technical report of the early 1990s, they now have what amounts to a "world or international oligopoly" over the heights of applied technology.32 For better or worse, the transnationals are at the institutional centre of late twentieth-century globalizing trends in the world economy.

In broad perspective, today's transnational corporations can be seen as spiritual descendants of such historic joint-stock enterprises as the English and Dutch East India companies, which played key roles in the earlier expansion of the European sea-borne empires. In a narrower institutional sense their history began in Europe, during the imperial high tide of the later nineteenth century – "Bayer of Germany in 1863; Nestlé of Switzerland in 1867; the Belgian Solvay in 1881; Michelin (France) in 1893; and Lever Brothers (United Kingdom) in 1890."33

For a variety of reasons – including the First World War, the Russian Revolution of 1917, and the Great Depression of the 1930s – the first four decades of the twentieth century were less hospitable to transnational corporate expansion than the last decades of the previous century. The fortunes of

---

* "Transnational" is the more general and analytically comprehensive term. "Multinational" implies an enterprise that is active in *many* countries. A transnational enterprise can be active in as few as two countries (i.e., more than one) or in as many countries (or national states) as there are.

the transnationals improved in the wake of the Second World War, when the "best-known phase of multinational growth was basically by American firms." This phase "began almost as soon as the Second World War ended in 1945 and continued to the end of the sixties." Starting in the early 1970s, a new wave of growth took place among multinational firms based in Western Europe and Japan. There were as well some new firms that "originated in developing countries," especially in Asia.[34] As already noted, however, of the more than 37,000 transnational corporations tabulated by the United Nations in the early 1990s, more than 33,000 were based in Western Europe, North America, and Japan. Control over the global heights of late twentieth-century applied technology is still concentrated in a comparatively small chunk of the world's geography.

Nevertheless, the transnational corporations of the world today are the most obvious institutional heirs of capitalism's historic capacity to deliver the goods of the machine civilization that (speaking metaphorically of course) everyone else wants. Their present habits – or organizational cultures – may not have a lot in common with the eighteenth-century liberal ideas of the Anglo-American bourgeoisie in which Christopher Farrell and others are still placing so much faith; they may still be very far from *global* corporations in any comprehensive sense; but they do now have interests and operations in many parts of the world beyond their home-country "triad" of Western Europe, North America, and Japan. And, as an inescapable practical matter, they wield a vast influence over just what globalization may or may not mean for everyone's future.

For some two and a half generations in the most recent past, it was possible to believe that there was another route to the technological rewards of the machine civilization – via the alternative model of industrialization that Soviet Russia tried to pioneer between 1917 and 1989. Yet, whatever the eventual fate of those democratic forms of socialism that accept the importance of capitalist mobilization, the revolutionary communist alternative has now been judged a failure by the people who tried it themselves. In this last decade of the twentieth century China and India (by far the two most populous countries in the world) have also made a peace of sorts with the transnational corporations, bringing them into their own economic and political calculations. For any current time frame that it makes sense even to think about, the world at large may not have to love the multinationals, but because their technology is what everyone really wants, it does have to conspire to live with them.

Table 4
The Seventy-five Largest Transnational Corporations, 1992
(By Home Country; Ranked by Foreign Assets)

UNITED STATES
Exxon
IBM
General Motors
Ford
General Electric
Mobil
Du Pont
Philip Morris
Chrysler
Dow Chemical
Xerox
Proctor & Gamble
Chevron
Texaco
Pepsico
Amoco
Eastman Kodak
ITT

JAPAN
Hitachi
Matsushita Electric
Toyota Motor Co.
Sony
Nissho Iwai
Toshiba
Honda
Bridgestone
Nissan Motor
Itachu Corporation
Sharp
Marubeni

NEC Corporation
Mitsui

GERMANY
Volkswagen
Siemens
Daimler Benz
Bayer
BASF
Hoechst
Veba
Robert Bosch
BMW

FRANCE
Alcatel Alsthom
Elf Aquitaine
Lyonnaise des Eaux
Total
Saint Gobain
Michelin
Rhône-Poulenc
Renault
Pechiney

UNITED KINGDOM
British Petroleum
Hanson
B.A.T. Industries
Grand Metropolitan
ICI
Glaxo Holdings
RTZ

SWITZERLAND
Nestlé
Asea Brown Boveri
Ciba-Geigy
Sandoz
Roche Holdings
Holderbank

CANADA
Seagram
Thomson Corporation
Alcan Aluminum

ITALY
Fiat
ENI

SWEDEN
Electrolux
Volvo

BELGIUM
Petrofina
Solvay

NETHERLANDS
Philips Electronics

U.K./NETHERLANDS
Royal Dutch Shell
Unilever

Source: United Nations, *World Investment Report 1994.*

CHAPTER THREE

TWISTS AND TURNS

THE NEW ECONOMIC FORCES, 1970–1995

"In the case of capitalism ... the left has recently discovered that it doesn't have an alternative."

Richard Rorty, 1994[1]

One chapter in the story of the globalization process over the past quarter-century is about how the Soviet model of industrialization came to fail. Yet the whole story has many more chapters, and like recent technological development, they move at a reckless pace – as if a videotape of an earlier whole century or more were run at fast forward.

The story is also about how the world economy had to cope with the dismantled European empires, and how "Germany and Japan, the defeated powers of the Second World War," became new "industrial giants."[2] It is about how the United States, which at the end of the Second World War was "the world's largest economy with industrial output greater than that of all other countries combined,"[3] inevitably lost its overwhelming dominance. It is about how some old European colonies became new petroleum-exporting countries, and about what happened in China after the death of Mao Zedong. It is about the early impact of the third and fourth waves of the industrial revolution and the appearance of new industrializing economies in such places as Singapore, South Korea, Thailand, and Hong Kong.

THE WORLD OF TWO ECONOMIC HALVES AFTER 1945

The story's immediate historical background – the quarter-century from 1945 to 1970 – is a key to what happened in the 1970s, 1980s, and early 1990s. The ironic point of departure is the rising fortunes of the global political and economic left at the end of the Second World War.

To start with, the birthplace of the alternative model of industrialization emerged from the war with fresh vigour and strength. The "European state that was most obviously victorious on VE-Day 1945 was the Soviet Union."[4]

After the fighting, "Moscow-trained Communists who had quite literally arrived in the baggage train of the Red Army"[5] established new versions of the alternative model in Bulgaria, Czechoslovakia, Hungary, Poland, Rumania, eastern Germany, and Tito's "nationalist" Yugoslavia between 1945 and 1949.

Then, on 1 October 1949, Mao Zedong proclaimed the birth of the communist People's Republic of China. After a long era of deep disarray, he told the world, "China has stood up!"[6] In February 1950 the new China and the Soviet Union signed a Treaty of Friendship, Alliance, and Mutual Aid. Soviet advisers poured in to help industrialize the most populous country in the world. Some thought the Chinese revolution would be "for the latter half of the twentieth century what the Russian Revolution was for the first half."[7]

Back in July 1945 the democratic socialist Labour party had already won a dramatic general election, even in the metropolis of the capitalist British empire. Clement Atlee formed a Labour government in the United Kingdom, and on 16 August the new government "announced an ambitious programme: nationalization of the coal industry and of the bank of England; social security; a national health service."[8]

This picture did have its complications. There were quite vast differences between socialism in the United Kingdom and other parts of Western Europe (which, having already industrialized, had no need of an alternative model) and communism in the Soviet Union and China.

In 1946 the self-confessed British "democratic Socialist" George Orwell wrote that it was "too early to say in just what way the Russian régime will destroy itself." But he believed that it "will either democratise ... or it will perish." If he "were compelled to choose between Russia and America ... I would always choose America."[9]

The United States itself, with the atomic bomb in one hand and a larger economy than the rest of the world combined in the other, was still home to "masses" who were "contented with capitalism."[10] Its largest business corporations had already begun their rapid postwar march to multinationalism, aggressively opening branch plants offshore. U.S. enterprise was playing a leading role in the economic recovery of Western Europe. And the U.S. Army was superintending a major political and economic restructuring in Japan.

It was nonetheless a stark fact, at this point, that in the world at large there were now two apparently credible rival approaches to trying to achieve the technological blessings of the machine civilization. Even in the middle of the 1960s the far from ideologically dogmatic Anglo-American economist Kenneth Boulding would pronounce that the world is divided into two economic halves, the socialist camp on the one side and the "free world" on the other. These two halves are by no means completely isolated ... but ... in some degree it may be said that each half of the economic world is pursuing a line of development that is largely separated from that of the other half.[11]

LEFT-RIGHT CYCLES AND THE THIRD WORLD

For all practical purposes the left in Western Europe and North America was part of the free world, not of the socialist camp. There was some marginal seepage at the fringes of serious politics (institutionalized most successfully in the communist parties of Italy and France, and sometimes the object of a paranoia that reached its heights in the McCarthy witch-hunt of the early 1950s in the United States), but the most potent moral conflict of the so-called Cold War was between "totalitarianism" and "democracy," not socialism and capitalism. After 1945 the earlier obscure democratic socialist writer Orwell became "an important guarantor, as he was one of the makers, of ... the Cold War consensus."[12]

Domestically, what the postwar British Labour party and its various Western European and (more liberal) North American analogues finally created was not the democratic socialism that even Orwell hoped would be possible. It was merely a democratic capitalist social welfare state. Government expenditures as a share of gross national product rose from 30 percent in 1938 to 44 percent in 1970 in the United Kingdom, and from 22 percent in 1940 to 35 percent in 1970 in the United States.[13]

Internationally, the British Labour party played another kind of role in creating a new politically independent third world – beyond, as it were, the first and second worlds of the two economic halves. In August 1947 the Labour government in the metropolis of the British empire proved that all its earlier talk about democracy, self-determination, and racial equality did have some truth in it by liberating the Indian subcontinent from the bonds of the British Raj.

Idealism was far from being the Labour government's only motivation. It faced harsh political pressures from the Indian National Congress and from the Muslim League, which would create the new state of Pakistan. Both India and Pakistan achieved independence on a first wave of decolonization that followed the war. The wave included the former British colonies of Ceylon (later called Sri Lanka) and Burma (which may or may not now be called Myanmar). It also included the former Dutch colony of Indonesia (the world's fourth most populous country in the 1990s). The Japanese wartime occupation of such places as Burma and Indonesia had helped weaken the old European imperial grip. The Dutch left Indonesia more reluctantly and less peacefully than the British left India, but by 1950 Indonesia was independent all the same.

By 1950 the right had started to reassert itself in Western Europe and North America; yet this only temporarily repressed a postwar global leftward surge that would carry on through to the end of the 1960s, or even into the middle of the 1970s. The first world's struggle against the second world became mixed up with decolonization in the third world. However, the early 1950s war in Korea (a former colony of Japan) was an odd case: Korea lacked a potent history of nationalist struggle against European imperialism – the sort of history the United States would soon be confronted with in the former French colony of Vietnam.

Burma, Ceylon, India, and Indonesia had set decisive precedents. By the time the old British Gold Coast in west Africa had become the new state of Ghana (and what is now Malaysia had joined the United Nations), in 1957, a second and unstoppable wave of postwar decolonization was in motion.

In 1958 tumult in Algeria brought domestic political upheaval to France. The French empire was dismantling itself as fast as the British empire. By 1959 the Belgian Congo was in turmoil. In 1960 seventeen "new states" (sixteen of which were in Africa) became members of the United Nations. There were four more in 1961, another six in 1962, two in 1963, three in 1964, another three in 1965, four in 1966, and two in 1968.

All told forty-one new states joined the United Nations during the 1960s. Many new third-world leaders said they were socialists. They aspired to disentangle themselves from the capitalism and foreign investment of the European empires from which they thought they were escaping. And they believed that government had a key role to play in Eric Hobsbawm's "'emerging' nation of today which sets about its own industrial revolution." Even in Western Europe and North America the resurgent conservative politicians of the 1950s typically gave way to leaders with more faith in government action. In the 1960s these progressive leaders increased public expenditures on the democratic capitalist social welfare states, which even the conservatives of the 1950s had not seriously tried to roll back.

TWO CRISES: BRETTON WOODS AND OPEC

In the 1970s new economic forces began to thwart the postwar global leftward movement in a much more fundamental way than the conservative resurgence of the 1950s had. For a while, however, it was possible to imagine that these new forces might be boosting the fortunes of the left still more.

In the first place, the multinational expansion of corporate America from 1945 to the end of the 1960s had been underpinned by a new international financial regime – created in the summer of 1944 by a body called the

United Nations Monetary and Financial Conference, which met at a 10,000-acre New England resort known as Bretton Woods. Though attended by forty-four different countries, the conference was largely masterminded by the United States and the United Kingdom: the imminent key first-world victors of the Second World War.

One crucial ingredient of the Bretton Woods agreement was the United States' commitment to stabilize the price of gold by purchasing whatever gold anyone wanted to sell at some thirty-five U.S. dollars an ounce.* This helped establish a predictable financial framework for the postwar first-world economy – and even a degree of (U.S.) government control over the financial heights of an emerging new (and post-colonial) form of global capitalism. It was not too hard for the United States to do, so long as it retained enough of the overwhelming global economic dominance it had stumbled upon in the immediate wake of the vast destruction wrought by the Second World War.

Yet it is easy to see in retrospect that this overwhelming degree of U.S. dominance could not possibly last. Serious trouble began to brew in the 1960s and reached crisis proportions at the height of the Vietnam War. On Sunday, 15 August 1971, Richard Nixon announced that his government was no longer prepared (or able) to provide a global financial "fulcrum" by guaranteeing the price of gold. Under the Bretton Woods regime the U.S. dollar had gradually become "virtually defenceless" against competitive "alterations in the par values of other currencies." What the Second World War destroyed had now been rebuilt. There was "no longer any need," as Nixon put it, "for the United States to compete with one hand tied behind her back." The announcement "precipitated an unprecedented series of world financial crises" and ultimately led to a new kind of anarchic and volatile free-market international financial system that is still with us today.[14]

Only five months before Nixon's fateful act, there had been a second sign of strange new directions. Coal had been the great energy resource of the first industrial revolution. In the second revolution of the machine civilization its place was usurped by electricity and oil. One reason for the great U.S. leap ahead of the United Kingdom in the early twentieth century was that the Americans initially had a great deal of oil within their own borders. After the First World War, in response to (mistaken) perceptions of the day about imminent domestic shortages, large U.S. oil corporations began to

---

* Institutionally, the Bretton Woods conference established the International Monetary Fund and what has become the World Bank. These Bretton Woods institutions have survived the subsequent U.S. abandonment of its commitment to stabilize the price of gold, though their influence and style of operation have inevitably changed.

take an interest in international supplies – particularly in a region misnamed by world inhabitants of the late twentieth century, "who keep calling the Near East the 'Middle East.'"[15]

Between the mid-1920s and the mid-1950s "U.S. companies, starting with no base, gained a dominant position in an area that was to hold the future of the world's oil supply." By the early 1950s seven major transnational corporations, five of which were based in the United States, controlled "98 percent of the world oil market."[16] Yet a particular variation on the postwar decolonization movement would soon start a dramatic chain of events. In 1960 four Middle Eastern states and the oil-rich South American nation of Venezuela formed a group known as the Organization of Petroleum Exporting Countries (OPEC). The group's objective was to pressure the transnational oil corporations into granting host-country governments a greater financial return on their oil resources.

At the time hardly anyone in the international oil business took this objective seriously, but within a mere decade circumstances in both world oil markets and the transnational industry had conspired to give OPEC real leverage. In May 1970 Libya managed to squeeze unusual concessions from one of several U.S.-based "independent" oil companies, now in competition with the "seven majors." In February 1971 OPEC at large had its first success in pressuring the transnationals to adopt price increases that boosted the public revenues of its member states:

> The adroit maneuvering of the OPEC nations ... aided by the vacillation of the American government, gave OPEC their first clear-cut victory over the West. They obtained what was considered at the time to be a large price increase: fifty cents a barrel. America's reign over world oil production was swiftly coming to an end.[17]

By the middle of the 1970s the OPEC nations included Algeria, Ecuador, Gabon, Indonesia, Iran, Iraq, Kuwait, Libya, Nigeria, Qatar, Saudi Arabia, the United Arab Emirates, and Venezuela.* Shortly after war broke out between Egypt and Israel in October 1973, production cutbacks and embargoes dictated by Arab governments (led by Saudi Arabia) threw world oil markets into crisis. Late in December 1973 the OPEC nations met in Iran and "announced a price hike ... OPEC's take was to be $7.00 a barrel, compared with $1.77 before the October War." The oil-producing countries

---

* All but Ecuador and Gabon were on board by the end of 1971. Ecuador was a full and Gabon an associate member by the end of 1973. Gabon became a full member in 1975. (*OPEC General Information and Chronology 1990*, 9–10.)

had now "seized control of the world's basic energy source."[18] The emerging global village would never be the same again.

NEW DIVERSITIES IN THE COLD WAR CAMPS

Ardent global left-wingers at the end of 1973 could still be forgiven for believing that both the Bretton Woods and OPEC crises would finally strengthen their hand. The deeper ironic truth was more complicated, and it ultimately pushed events in another direction. One reason for the United States' inability to keep on underwriting the government-stabilized Bretton Woods financial framework was the spectacular if not exactly surprising 1960s economic recovery in West Germany and Japan (both of which had in some degree been politically and economically restructured by the United States in the wake of the Second World War). In the new atmosphere the whole of Western Europe began to reassert itself.

"Fifteen years from now," the French economic journalist Jean-Jacques Servan-Schreiber had warned in his late 1960s book *Le Défi Américain*, "it is quite possible that the world's third greatest industrial power, just after the United States and Russia, will not be Europe, but *American industry in Europe.*"[19] Large European (and Japanese) business corporations rose to the challenge, mimicking the American multinationalism of the immediate postwar period.

As in earlier cases, the "hallmark of multinational as distinct from 'international' groups" was "that the multinational model involves the functional replication of mini-parent companies in one host country after another."[20] Just as U.S. companies had earlier opened branch plants in Europe (while the U.S. Army maintained a military occupation of Japan until 1952), European and Japanese companies began to open branch plants in the United States. In a dramatic turn of events, by the late 1970s the United States had become "the world's largest host country" for "foreign direct investment."[21]

In some hesitant respects corporate Europe was picking up where it had left off during the high point of imperial expansion in the late nineteenth and early twentieth centuries. Having forsworn militarism for economic competition, Japan was renovating its own earlier Asian counter-imperialism – with some pregnant wider implications.

One key upshot was a new strain of competitive pluralism in the economic leadership of the capitalist first world. The overwhelming postwar dominance of the United States rapidly gave way to a new *ad hoc* regime, embracing the globe's several largest national economies. The United States found it had to cease acting as a sergeant-major ... [I]t had no option but to share the stage and, indeed, to plead for the co-operation of Germany and Japan (constituting the Group of 3 or G-3) and, to a much lesser extent, of the British, the French, the Italians, and the Canadians who constitute the other members of the Group of 7 (G-7).[22]

The rising new pluralism, on the other hand, was not confined to the capitalist first world. In the late 1960s Servan-Shreiber had written: "Ten years ago people did not ask *if* the Russians would reach the American standard of living, but when they would go beyond it," but by 1968 it was clear that "Soviet agriculture remains petrified in the kolkhoz system and commerce in the state-owned stores. The 'great leap forward' took place in the United States."[23]

As early as 1960 Mao Zedong's China had raised its own doubts about the alternative colonialism of the alternative model of industrialization, and requested its Russian advisers and technicians to leave. In the 1960s and early 1970s Mao led China through its own stormy Chinese socialist adventures. In the end these did not bring the coveted machine civilization any closer than the Russians had.

After Mao's death in 1976 the leadership that finally succeeded him in the Communist Party of China (CPC) took a radically fresh look at what was happening – in China, in the Soviet Union, and in the world at large. In December 1978,

> after making an in-depth analysis of both international and domestic economic construction experiences and the overall international situation, the CPC Central Committee formulated a major strategic decision on introducing economic reform, invigorating domestic economy and opening to the outside world ... The introduction of various forms of the household contract responsibility system, which linked remuneration to output, stimulated the enthusiasm of farmers for developing commodity production ... At the same time China began establishing special economic zones and opened 14 coastal port cities.[24]

It was the late 1980s (or even the early 1990s) before what all this meant started to become entirely clear. But this time it was the international socialist camp that would never be the same again. As early as the late 1970s the once-rising fortunes of the old global political and economic left had seriously begun to wane.

MULTINATIONAL ADVENTURES IN THE LESS-DEVELOPED COUNTRIES

The key parts of the outside world that China began opening to in the late 1970s and early 1980s were the headquarters of the multinational or transnational corporations, in Western Europe, North America, and Japan. And here China was joining a wider trend. In the summer of 1978 the U.S. business press had reported the beginnings of a great "shift in the relations between the 'old' economic world and the 'new.'"

> [The] catalyst for the current upheaval in world economic power was the most jarring event of the 1970s – the quadrupling of oil prices in 1974 by the Organization of Petroleum Exporting Countries (OPEC). This triggered three fundamental changes: a sharp slowing in world economic growth, a slowing in the rise of world trade, and an increase in the productivity of labour relative to capital that is strengthening the economies of advanced developing countries, such as South Korea and Brazil.[25]

In almost all respects this shift in relations is still in progress today, but "the most jarring event of the 1970s" illuminated some crucial aspects of the broader logic behind the accelerated globalizing trends of the late twentieth century. Even in the high-technology era of the third and fourth industrial revolutions, labour remained a potent factor of production. Crushing new cost and competitive pressures induced by the OPEC oil shocks gave transnational corporations good reason to take a fresh and highly rational interest in less-developed third-world countries, where sufficiently skilled workers were willing to accept much lower wages than workers in the developed first world.

China was also not the only less-developed place where accumulated experience was drawing attention to the weaknesses of industrial growth strategies that were dominated by government and politics – inside and outside the Soviet Union. Pressed ahead, in many cases, by the new anarchic free-market international financial system, other third-world leaders began to court the transnational corporations and foreign direct investment that they had earlier tried to avoid.

Over the short term, dramatic improvements in transportation, communications, and information technology made it possible to spread industrial production serving first-world markets in a more geographically dispersed fashion. The result was that first-world consumers increasingly purchased products made by or for first-world corporations in third-world countries. At the same time, the global economic doldrums of the 1970s, followed by the great recession of the early 1980s, starkly raised the prospect that the most promising long-term future for transnational corporate growth lay not in the mature economies of Western Europe, North America, and Japan, but in the emerging markets of the less-developed countries, where vast populations still needed the basic consumer goods of the machine civilization.

A United Nations technical report of the late 1980s spelled out the ultimate consequences of this broader logic. "Recent changes in the policies, laws and regulations of developing countries," the UN authors observed, "have confirmed the trend, apparent since the early 1980s, towards the liberalization of policies on" foreign direct investment. "Efforts to remove some of the conditions on entry and operations of" transnational corporations "have been complemented by attempts to render more efficient the administrative procedures for admission and for the grant of incentives to those corporations."[26]

In this process the politically anachronistic economic structure of George Orwell's old Western imperial system – "which we all live on and which we denounce when there seems to be no danger of its being altered"[27] – had ironically begun to crack at last.

The Ambiguities of Recent Third-World Growth

More than anything else, this ironic cracking is at the bottom of the monumental change that the historic globalization process is now bringing to the world economy. And we have still only begun to understand it.

Some first-world analysts argue that too much stress can be placed on the strategic attractions of low third-world labour costs. "Obviously," the U.S. political scientist Earl Fry urged in the early 1990s, "if wages were the sole criterion for locating industrial facilities, then Haiti would already be the industrial capital of the world."[28]

Third-world analysts, however, have another point of view. According to the Brazilian politician Rubens Ricupero, "developing countries are always suspicious that, when one speaks about uniform labour standards to give workers everywhere a decent treatment ... he may be trying to nullify one of the few competitive advantages they have: the low cost of manpower."[29]

Still other critics have stressed that even with this advantage not all developing countries have benefited uniformly from the symbiosis between transnational corporations and the third world that finally began to develop in the 1970s and 1980s.

To start with the most positive side of the ledger, the earliest new third-world capitalist economic stars were the four Asian "tigers" of Hong Kong, Singapore, South Korea, and Taiwan – all of which enjoyed strategic historical ties to one or more of Japan, the old European empires, and the United States. Then, by the early 1990s, the CPC's "major strategic decision" of

1978 actually had begun to turn China into "the emerging economic powerhouse of the 21st century."[30] Dynamic development in such other Asian places as Indonesia, Malaysia, and Thailand (and, most recently, at least some parts of India) was "shifting the world centre of economic gravity."[31]

On the other hand, though "Chile had enjoyed a decade of solid economic growth"[32] by this point, even today the two Latin American demographic heavyweights, Brazil and Mexico, have still not exactly met recurrent bursts of high expectations. A few parts of the Middle East have grown rich on oil royalties without acquiring a real industrial capacity of their own. And despite some major liberalization of national development policies by some African governments, most of tropical Africa has so far gained almost nothing from the new globalizing trends.

The Volatility of Emerging Markets

It would be quaint to imagine that changes as monumental as those unleashed by the new economic forces of the past quarter-century can ever unfold quietly. Since the late 1970s, enthusiasm for the emerging markets of less-developed countries on the part of both transnational corporations and first-world investors has waxed and waned, through several awkward boom-and-bust cycles. By the early 1980s the initial excitement faltered, and the anarchic free-market international financial system had saddled assorted third-world places with massive new piles of debt.

Investment in "developing countries" began to pick up again in the later 1980s, reaching new heights in the early 1990s. The "outstanding feature" of global investment flows

> during 1992 and 1993 was their considerable increase into developing countries ... In fact, between 1986 ... and 1993, investment flows into developing countries increased five-fold ... flows into developing countries in 1993 were the same as total world flows in 1986 ... South, East and South-East Asia as well as Latin America and the Caribbean – but not Africa – participated in this increase.[33]

The collapse of the Mexican peso in late 1994 and early 1995 precipitated another bust of sorts in the cycle, especially in Latin America and the Caribbean. While several new "emerging stock markets" were badly "battered," however, to the "multinationals' patient capital" this latest trouble is apparently "just a bump in the road." At the edge of the twenty-first century many European, Japanese, and U.S. companies "have invested so heavily in emerging markets that they are locked in to a long term view."[34]

Large and small U.S. multinational firms are now concerned that

Washington's too-protracted political hangover from the 1960s is giving Japanese and French firms dangerous new economic advantages on the old military battlefields of Southeast Asia. In response, by the early summer of 1995 the Clinton administration had finally started to move on the still-agonizing issue of normalizing U.S. relations with Vietnam. And, according to the United Nations, by this point there were already some 2,850 new transnational corporations *headquartered* in developing countries themselves – including 57 firms in Pakistan, 187 in India, 379 in China, 500 in Hong Kong, 566 in Brazil, and 1,049 in South Korea.[35]

THE FIRST WORLD AND GLOBAL INTEGRATION

It would no doubt be wrong for first-world inhabitants to become unduly alarmed about what the globalizing trends of the late twentieth century imply for their collective fate. For the moment, Asia is the obvious heartland of the new symbiosis between developing countries and transnational corporations. And such first-world critics as the U.S. economist Paul Krugman have urged that "Asia's spectacular growth is suspect because it was achieved simply by using more people to make things rather than by making production more efficient."[36]

Whatever else, the higher management or ultimate control of the processes of technological innovation that drive the third and fourth industrial revolutions is still largely concentrated within Western Europe, North America, and the first modernized Asian economic base in Japan. In the 1970s and even the 1980s it was often argued that this implied some new international division of labour. Traditional low-technology industrial employment would gravitate towards low-wage, third-world locations, and be replaced by new high-technology employment in high-wage countries of the first world.

In manufacturing at least, this prospect has dimmed in the later 1980s and 1990s. Much of the traditional, low-technology textile industry (the first goods-producing sector to be industrialized in eighteenth-century Britain) has in fact gravitated towards low-wage, third-world locations. But so have some elements of much newer and more sophisticated forms of manufacturing activity – in electronics and related fields. It is not really necessary, it seems, to pay high wages to those who merely assemble high-technology products. Malaysia, for instance, is one third-world location that "has been able to develop an impressive array of high-technology exports." Though low wages were an initial attraction, as "technologies progressed and wages rose," transnational corporations "responded by automating their facilities in Malaysia and diversifying" into other high-technology "assembly operations."[37] For some of the original third-world economic stars among the Asian tigers, there has been still deeper progress. Having "moved years ago from a low-wage economy where workers churned out shoes, textiles, small TVs, and cheap cars," South Korea is now "bidding to become one of the world's leading producers of high-tech goods ... the first nation to truly establish itself as an advanced industrial power since the emergence of Japan.'"38

The new information and communications technologies of the microelectronics revolution are nonetheless crucial keys to the administration, management, and marketing processes involved in "global economic integration." And the first world's current oligopolistic grip on technological innovation probably does give its expanding higher-order service sectors some form of leadership role in whatever integration of this sort may continue to take place in the foreseeable future. This theme is at the heart of much of the controversy about globalization today, and we will return to it more than once in the rest of this book. A few initial points of clarification, however, are appropriate here.

Financial Markets and Shallow Integration

It seems clear that the commanding heights of world financial markets (which do so much to guide and control the rest of economic life) mark the place where the new technologies have spawned the most dramatic degree of global integration: "The truly global firm – whose operations are unconstrained by the limitations of time or space – appears to have evolved furthest in financial services, such as securities, insurance and payments services."39

Money can now be electronically transferred around the world with breathtaking speed, and it is no doubt true that the free-market financial system bequeathed by the Bretton Woods crisis of the early 1970s has helped liberate global financial decisions from the narrowest interests of entrenched first-world élites. Critics also worry, however, about the increasing volatility and anarchy of this system. Some believe that, "with its power amplified by incredible leaps in communications and information technology," the system is now breeding "market players" who "will become a new class of stateless legislators," with the "power of the purse" to "check governments' ability to tax, spend, borrow, or depreciate their debts through inflation." The sudden collapse of the United Kingdom's 233-year-old Barings PLC merchant bank early in 1995, as a result of the actions of one twenty-eight-year-old, British-born, stateless legislator in the bank's Singapore branch, has illustrated "a dark side" of global financial integration "that is only now starting to emerge."40

In goods production and consumption activities, which more obviously affect the great majority of the world's population, it also seems clear that the increasing geographic diffusion of first-world lifestyles is promoting increasing degrees of what United Nations analysts call "shallow integration." Since the end of the Second World War, the increasing "size and geographical scope of cross-border market exchanges" – reflected in financial activity and foreign direct investment, trade in goods (and increasingly some services), and even modest but rising degrees of international labour mobility – have prompted "a clear trend towards more integrated world markets."[41]

In at least some senses one lightbulb, or vacuum cleaner, or refrigerator, or television set, or telephone, or tape recorder is quite like another. And (though even this is the subject of increasing debate) there are no doubt a few shallow respects in which technology itself has already locked the planet into some degree of movement "towards a more global and single-system society," where Bali is "only climatically different from Ballymurphy."[42] As George Orwell observed as long ago as the 1930s, the spread of the machine civilization around the globe cannot help but "make one part of the world indistinguishable from another."

Deep Integration and Regionalism in the Triad

There is much more controversy (and uncertainty) about what United Nations analysts call "deep integration" or "integrated international production." Ultimately this raises the question of Cyrus Freidheim's global corporation, which at the moment remains "largely a fiction."

As early as the late 1970s the "short-lived 'world car' concept" (which envisioned assembling automobiles from uniform components made in many different parts of the globe) had raised the prospect that "totally standardised 'world production'" was an approach to achieving the cost savings required to diffuse the machine civilization throughout the planet. But then the demise of the Bretton Woods system and the so-called second oil shock of 1979 pushed first-world transnational corporations in new directions.[43] In the 1980s there was much strategic corporate mixing and mingling in Europe, North America, and – to a lesser extent – Japan.

By the middle of the 1990s the U.S.-based Ford Motor Company, whose current chief executive officer was born and raised in the United Kingdom, had launched the ambitious "Ford 2000" strategy. Echoing the world-car concept, it will merge the corporation's separate European, American, South American, and Asian branch operations in an effort to achieve major cost savings by producing what amounts to a single line of "global cars." If this strategy succeeds, it will likely enough have a startling demonstration effect, but as matters stand, more than one critic is wondering "how you develop an Escort for five different continents and keep the cost low."[44]

One obvious and fundamental constraint on the widest future of such integrated international production is that, even with all the recent mixing and mingling in the European/North American/Japanese triad, the commanding heights of technological innovation in the first world remain politically and culturally divided. There are, for example, still significant differences even between the capitalist business cultures of North America and Western Europe (especially the continental Europe that does not include the United Kingdom).

The Japanese in particular have evolved their own unique approach. And since the late 1980s there have been new domestic voices urging Japan to end its "50 years of 'unnatural' membership in the Western community." Many Japanese today apparently want "more freedom from the United States" (Japan's primary patron and sponsor in the first world, as it were, since the end of the Second World War). Even the chief executive officer of the Fuji Xerox Company is talking about "re-Asianization." The Japanese modernizers who attacked the Tokugawa shogunate in the middle of the nineteenth century coined the slogan *"datsu-ah, ny-o"* ("leave Asia, enter the West"). At least some of their descendants now have a new reverse slogan: *"datsu-o, nyu-ah."*[45]

Whatever transnational corporations in Japan or Western Europe or North America or any other region of the globe may do, at the edge of the twenty-first century the world economy is still a vast distance away from any comprehensive kind of deep integration. If the "great idea" of an authentic global corporation ever is to become a reality, it seems clear enough that it will not happen overnight.

Table 5
Share of Major Regions and Countries in World Production
(Gross Domestic Product at 1980 Purchasing Power; Percentage of World Total)

Country/Region	1967	1973	1980	1986	1989
United States	25.7	22.8	20.9	20.9	20.8
Western Europe	25.9	25.3	23.9	22.4	22.2
Japan	5.6	7.0	7.2	7.5	7.8
South/East/Southeast Asia*	11.0	11.8	13.8	17.4	19.3
Latin America	7.1	7.7	8.8	8.0	7.5
Africa**	3.1	3.2	3.4	3.2	3.0
Rest of the world	21.7	22.1	22.2	20.5	19.4

* Including China
** Except South Africa

Source: G. van Liemt, in United Nations, *World Investment Report 1994.*

Table 6
Average Hourly Wages in the International Clothing Industry, 1992
(Deutschmarks – Including Social Costs)

Germany (West)	27.30
France	15.81
United Kingdom	13.77
United States	11.92
Hong Kong	5.25
Mexico (U.S. border)	2.53
Morocco	1.81
Malaysia	1.44
Jamaica	1.27
India	0.52

Source: R. Jungnickel, in United Nations, *World Investment Report 1994.*

CHAPTER FOUR

THE FIRST POLITICAL FALLOUT

FREE-MARKET REFORM, THE END OF THE COLD WAR, EUROPEAN UNION, AND THE NEW TRADE AGREEMENTS

"What is progressive today and conducive to freedom may be false tomorrow and a hindrance to freedom."

Franz Neumann, 1953[1]

Just where economics ends and politics begins in the globalization process of today is not easy to say. It does seem, however, that a large part of recent political debate and action has been a response to the new global economic forces of the 1970s, 1980s, and earlier 1990s (even if these same forces have sometimes been political creations themselves).

One underlying response of this sort virtually everywhere has been a sea change – or several different kinds of sea change – in "the intellectual climate of opinion, which determines the unthinking preconceptions of most people and their leaders, their conditioned reflexes to one course of action or another."[2]

The Bretton Woods crisis, the OPEC oil shocks, the tightening transnational grip on technological innovation, and the third and fourth waves of the continuing industrial revolution have all contributed to a new political mood of free-market reform – in the first and even what used to be the second worlds, as well as in the developing countries.

This is what Christopher Farrell points to when he talks about the "triumph of the liberal ideas of the bourgeoisie." Here again, however, my argument is that it would be wrong to jump to conclusions. It is particularly misleading to imagine any exact equation between free-market reform in the world at large and the recent, almost evangelical revival of the ideology of the private sector in English-speaking countries (especially in the United Kingdom and the United States).

THE AMBIGUITIES OF FREE-MARKET REFORM

According to a key text of the late 1970s, the new Anglo-American free-market mood has drawn on the culturally specific gospel of "economic freedom and limited government" advocated in two "documents published in the same year, 1776" – Adam Smith's *The Wealth of Nations* and the U.S. Declaration of Independence. This gospel (or so the argument goes) "produced a golden age in both Great Britain and the United States in the nineteenth century."[3] Its late twentieth-century revival coincided with the end of both the British empire and the postwar global hegemony of the United States – summarized for mass television audiences by the Iranian hostage incidents that so disfigured the Carter presidency.

The revived gospel called for a return to the values of the Anglo-American golden age. It also claimed to explain the slow economic growth and increasingly rampant inflation of the 1970s and early 1980s. The root of the trouble was that the tide of "economic freedom and limited government" had subsequently turned "toward Fabian socialism and New Deal liberalism ... fostering a change in the direction of British policy early in the twentieth century, and in U.S. policy after the Great Depression." By the late 1970s the "experience of recent years – slowing growth and declining productivity – raises a doubt whether private ingenuity can continue to overcome the deadening effects of government control if we continue to grant ever more power to government."[4]

The gospel's advocates believed that it was time for the tide to turn again. And it did turn enough to put Margaret Thatcher into 10 Downing Street in 1979 and Ronald Reagan into the White House in 1981. Thatcher never won a majority of the popular vote in any of her three British election victories. And Reagan never won support from a majority of the voting-age population in the United States. But only two years after Bill Clinton's 1992 presidential victory for the more centrist "new" Democrats, the heirs of Ronald Reagan showed renewed strength in the U.S. congressional elections of 1994. Nonetheless, whatever the future of domestic politics in either the United States or the United Kingdom may bring, there are increasingly apparent limits to the global reach of the culturally specific Anglo-American gospel of free-market reform, even given the international influence of the English language and the continuing size and strength of the U.S. economy.

At least until quite recently, the gospel's most ardent advocates explained Asia's first successful modernized economic base by arguing that the Japanese had also "adopted the policies of Adam Smith."[5] A more compelling case can be made for the view that what the Japanese have in fact borrowed from Anglo-American culture is the seventeenth- and early eighteenth-century protectionist policy tradition of mercantilism, which Adam Smith attacked in *The Wealth of Nations*. Japan's most potent legacy to the new industrializing economies of Asia (including China) is a historically new and cross-cultural "happy marriage of Confucius and Henry Ford."[6]

This view helps explain the continuing late twentieth-century dispute over free trade between Japan and the United States. As Chalmers Johnson ("America's most penetrating, provocative analyst of Japan's political economy") has maintained for more than two decades now, "Japan's politico-economic system differs far more from the Western model than most Westerners" realize. Here as elsewhere outside the United States and the United Kingdom, the neoclassical economics of which Adam Smith is the founding father is not always a "useful tool for understanding the world" today.[7]

In the still wider realms of the developing countries, the political climate of liberalization induced by the economic changes of the past quarter-century has in a number of respects amounted to little more than a new willingness to do business with first-world transnational corporations, which hold so many keys to the technologies of the machine civilization that everyone wants.

Even in the middle of the 1990s China claimed to be

> establishing a socialist market economy based on the following fundamental principles: the internal unification of public ownership and the market economy, effective state macro-regulation and control, market mechanisms playing a basic role in the allocation of resources, and the distribution system giving priority to efficiency and due consideration to fairness.[8]

A table accompanying this explanation shows the progress in meeting these goals between 1978 and 1992 in the dramatically rising numbers of Chinese-manufactured refrigerators, television sets, tape recorders, and cameras. (And in the 1980s "China's growth climbed rapidly to a 10 percent annual rate," declined briefly to "4 percent" in 1988 and 1989 – "a level all Western countries would still regard as a boom" – and then "re-accelerated to 7 percent in 1991.")[9]

By the early 1990s India had begun to liberalize its national development policies, and this has lately attracted enthusiastic investment by transnational corporations based in Western Europe and North America. However, there are still "limits on how far foreign investors can go." At the state level of government "you still have to go through the same old socialist rigmarole."[10]

In Singapore, which currently "has the highest reliance of almost any country" in the world on transnational corporations, the government has "also set up a number of public enterprises" to promote economic activities "considered to enhance the country's future competitive advantage." The "public sector in Singapore accounts for a substantial proportion" of gross domestic product. Oblivious to the principles of *The Wealth of Nations*, governments in both South Korea and Taiwan have taken "a strong lead in targeting industries for technology development." And they have used transnational corporations "primarily in furthering the acquisition of technology and the development of local innovative capabilities."[11]

THE END OF THE COLD WAR

It is worth remembering the limitations of the neoclassical economics that descend from Adam Smith in contemplating another, highly dramatic political response to the new economic forces – the collapse of the Soviet Union and the accompanying end of the Cold War between the first and second worlds, in the fateful year of 1989.

In the United States, *Time* magazine had noted the beginnings of some movement in this direction as early as March 1978. Recognizing "the global advances socialism has made in the decades following World War II," the magazine observed: "Today, self-proclaimed socialists of one variety or another rule 53 of the world's sovereign states, controlling 39% of its territory and 42% of its population." Yet it also stressed that, ironically, "at the very moment of its spectacular advances, socialism faces profound new crises of its own."[12]

China's first steps towards a new "socialist market economy" nine months later suggested just how profound these crises were. Some half-dozen years after this, in April 1985, Mikhail Gorbachev launched a parallel (though rather different) process in the Soviet Russian birthplace of the alternative model of industrialization itself.

It is still far too early for balanced judgments about the short twentieth-century history of the Union of Soviet Socialist Republics, but it is probably worth recalling that it could claim some achievements. In 1961 the U.S.S.R., not the U.S.A., had put the world's first manned space ship into orbit. In 1978 even *Time* magazine had sardonically acknowledged that "in six decades a war-shattered society in the earliest stages of industrialization has been transformed into a military superpower that produces more steel, crude oil, manganese and honey than the U.S."[13]

Yet, whatever its achievements, by the 1980s there was a growing consensus even inside the Soviet Union that the alternative model of industrialization had two hopeless flaws. To start with, it bred a totalitarian system that put everything – economy, politics, and culture – into the hands of government, or the state. On its bottom line the state is merely "a human community that (successfully) claims the *monopoly of the legitimate use of physical force* within a given territory."[14] And it is not surprising that, regardless of its intentions, a system that puts everything into such hands should degenerate into a sinister exercise in the abuse of physical force.

The alternative model's second (and not necessarily related) flaw was that, after more than two generations, it could still not deliver anything like the machine-civilization consumer goods enjoyed in the first world. It could only produce unreliable supplies of "soap the size of a Chiclet" and "cameras with lenses like dumbbells."[15] In retrospect this was not surprising either. Karl Marx himself had not imagined that socialist governments would try to industrialize non-industrial societies. In 1987 the maverick Yugoslavian political writer Milovan Djilas argued:

> It is clear from both theory and practice that Communism was (and could only be) moderately effective as a transition from feudal/semi-colonial formations to industrial-national ones; and then only on the understanding that it is inappropriate, destructive, and hopeless as a long-term and lasting economic and social creation.[16]

As if he had suddenly discovered George Orwell's 1946 judgment that the Soviet Union must democratize or perish, in the last half of the 1980s Gorbachev courageously tried to deal with both these flaws while preserving at least the façade of the communist experiment that Lenin had created. Why he failed – where China appears to have succeeded in a vaguely related quest – is (in some quarters) still a subject of ardent debate.

A cynic might note that China's official contribution to "1989" was the crushing of thousands of mostly unarmed political protesters in Beijing on 4 June. While Gorbachev may have dithered too much over the Soviet transition to a socialist market economy, his commitment to democratizing the totalitarian state was real enough to spark the collapse of the communist satellite regimes in Eastern Europe. The process culminated when "without plan or forethought" East German authorities, pressed by more "and more people ... moving onto the streets and out of the country," opened the Berlin Wall in November 1989.[17] At this point no one could doubt that the Cold War was over.

In the early 1990s the Soviet Union itself collapsed into the non-communist and formally democratic Russian Federation, under President Boris Yeltsin – an early critic of Gorbachev's dithering over free-market reforms. Reflecting a parallel liberation from the much earlier Russian land-borne empire, the new federation was surrounded by such other newly independent non-communist states (and former components of the U.S.S.R.) as Estonia, Belarus, the Ukraine, Georgia, Uzbekistan, and the Kyrgyz Republic.

Almost overnight the old second world had virtually disappeared. The first world's transnational corporations acquired yet another set of new free-market frontiers. First-world workers were confronted with yet another source of low-wage global competition. But the economic circumstances of the vast majority of the inhabitants of the former Union of Soviet Socialist Republics actually got worse.[18] By 1993 the new Russian Federation was only the eleventh-largest national economy on the planet – after China, Canada, Spain, and Brazil.*

THE NEW EUROPE

U.S. Secretary of State James A. Baker's comment on the events of 1989 was that the Russians were now "singing out of our hymnbook."[19] As Christopher Farrell's urgings about the triumph of the liberal values of the bourgeoisie suggest, other North Americans still tend to see the essential thrust of recent changes in global politics in a similar way.

The Western Europe whose early imperial expansion first created the modern new world, however, has begun to fashion its own political response to the economic changes of the 1970s, 1980s, and earlier 1990s. Here there is considerable evidence that, while the hymnbook may have a similar cover, there are rather different hymns inside.

As long ago as 1947 George Orwell was struggling with his last book of fiction, *Nineteen Eighty-Four* – a bleak, dystopian fantasy about a hopeless totalitarian future. But he took some time out to comment on politics in the real world for a small magazine in New York. Reflecting on the ruins of the Second World War, he suggested that Europe might be "finished and that in the long run some better form of society will arise in India or China." He added, speaking personally, that "a Socialist United States of Europe seems to me the only worth-while political objective today."[20]

Even in the 1940s this was hardly a vision unique to Orwell. With or without the socialist ideological prefix, it had forward-looking attractions for the coming age that would see the dismantling of the European sea-borne

---

* Based on *The World Bank Atlas*'s "standard measure of GNP," reported in the second table after the prologue in this book. According to the alternative "purchasing power parity" measure of GNP, discussed at somewhat greater length in chapter 6 below, the Russian Federation qualifies as one of the world's ten largest national economies.

empires. And that age had already begun with the independence of India, proclaimed at about the same time that Orwell's article appeared in print.

In May 1950, only a few months after the Soviet Union and Mao Zedong's new China had signed their Treaty of Friendship, Alliance and Mutual Aid, the French foreign minister Robert Schuman advanced a scheme for a European coal and steel community. It was "the most imaginative proposal that postwar Europe had yet heard and the one from which all subsequent progress toward European integration stemmed."[21] France, West Germany, Italy, Belgium, the Netherlands, and Luxembourg duly established the European Coal and Steel Community in 1951.

In 1957 the same "inner six" formed the broader but still loose and altogether unpolitical Common Market, or European Economic Community. Orwell's home country of the United Kingdom applied for membership in 1961, but the French president, Charles de Gaulle, vetoed the application in January 1963 – still remembering that during the Second World War Britain had "preferred a secondary status within the Anglo-American alliance to the role of Europe's defender."[22] Eventually de Gaulle ("Europe's last great political figure")[23] died, in November 1970. And by January 1973 the inner six had been joined by Denmark, Ireland, and the United Kingdom.

In the early 1980s, pressed by "the higher cost of energy imports ... the ∴ second OPEC price shock and the loss of export markets due to rising domestic prices and recessions in several trading partners," the European Community "as a whole and several of its larger members" confronted "a sharp decline in their current account balances."[24] In this atmosphere the "Europeans ... sought a strategy that would lower the domestic costs of goods and services" by creating new "potential for economies of scale" and by "expanding the size of the potential market available to producers while lowering or removing the political, economic, and legal barriers to trade" inside Europe itself.[25]

The search culminated in late 1985 and early 1986 with a document known as the Single European Act. By this point the full members of the European Community had expanded to an even dozen, with the addition of Greece in 1981 and then of Spain and Portugal in 1986. The Single European Act launched a process of much tighter economic, and even a significant degree of political, integration among the twelve member states. The process was scheduled to reach a decisive initial stage of implementation by 1992.

Despite recurrent bumps in the road, fresh commitments agreed upon at Maastricht in the Netherlands at the end of 1991 kept the process on track. Despite still more bumps in various roads, on 1 January 1995 Austria, Finland, and Sweden became full members.

By the middle of the 1990s a new kind of European union was in fact more or less in place, even if its future was said to be both "very different from the past and very different from what people are imagining now."[26]

One of the most unsettling bumps along the road toward European integration during the late 1980s and early 1990s was the end of the Cold War — and the collapse of the communist regimes in Eastern Europe. West Germany had already become the Common Market's strongest national economy. The subsequent reunification of the old eastern and western parts of the country created a "new, unified Germany" which — while not without its problems — was even more "indisputably the most important economic actor"[27] in the new European Union (EU).

This development may in turn have increased the comparative hesitancy that has marked the United Kingdom's participation in European integration, ever since it was finally admitted to the Common Market in the 1970s.* The United Kingdom continues to place a high value on "the excellent and unique and close and warm relationship we enjoy with the U.S."[28] Even in the middle of the 1990s there were signs of "creeping anti-Europeanism"[29] in British politics, and the "Anglo-Saxon version" of the new Europe's future remains rather different from "the Continental conception."[30]

Margaret Thatcher's British government was nonetheless a significant force in the European integration planning of the 1980s, abetted by something of a "rightward shift of the ideological center of gravity"[31] in Belgium, Denmark, the Netherlands, and West Germany during the same period. To a significant enough extent, the new European Union reflects wider trends towards free-market reform in the world at large. The current consensus seems to be that some rigorously "social democratic or neocorporatist Europe, redistributing to the 'losers' as markets become freer, is improbable."[32]

At the same time, the integrated Europe of the 1990s does have an explicit social dimension, including a Charter of Fundamental Social Rights to which all member states except George Orwell's old home country of the United Kingdom** have agreed.[33] And it is hard to square any sense of limit-

---

* "Thinking Europe is an un-British activity. Those who do it (even as consenting adults in private) risk being stigmatized as 'Eurointellectuals' — a neologism which neatly combines two things the British deeply mistrust." (Timothy Garton Ash, in the *Times Literary Supplement*, 5 May 1995, 3.)

** By the spring of 1995 Tony Blair, leader of the opposition Labour party (which Orwell supported in his day), had made clear that a new Labour government in the United Kingdom would endorse the charter. At least one side of Labour generally has been more pro-Europe than the Conservatives.

ed government with the dense cluster of supra-national European institutions concentrated in the Belgian city of Brussels today. Whatever it may become, the new Europe is not an enterprise that could be easily deduced from the particular free-market mind of Adam Smith.

THE NEW REGIONAL TRADE AGREEMENTS

Back in 1947 another of Orwell's real-world observations (which also found a particular fictional expression in *Nineteen Eighty-Four*) had raised the forbidding long-term prospect of "the division of the world among two or three vast super-states, unable to conquer one another and unable to be overthrown by any internal rebellion."[34]

The most obvious beginnings of such ominous creations in the late 1940s were in the U.S.A. and the U.S.S.R., but even at that time Orwell specified that his countervailing concept of a democratic socialist "United States of Europe," in order to "hold its own ... must include Africa and the Middle East"[35] – albeit under radically decolonized circumstances of "complete equality with the European peoples."*

It says something about the extent to which current trends are still embedded in a longer and deeper historical process that conceptions vaguely similar to Orwell's have figured at the edges of the late twentieth-century globalization debate. The recent more or less working example of the European Union has been provocative, and by 1975 the so-called Lomé Convention of the European Economic Community had erected a "complex structure of trade and aid support for almost the whole of Africa and a score of small communities, mostly islands, in the Caribbean and the Pacific,"[36] as a result of incremental efforts to square Europe's integrated future with its imperial past.

At the edge of the twenty-first century it is easy to project this European-based north-south pattern and envision at least three potential super-states, each anchored by one geographic piece of the first-world triad of Western Europe, North America, and Japan. Some observers have read various regional trade agreements that have arisen in response to the new economic forces in this light. Others, however, have maintained that the key trade agreement of the late twentieth century has been the Uruguay Round of the global General Agreement on Tariffs and Trade (GATT), which, like Orwell's super-states, has its own origins in the late 1940s.

---

* Somewhat idealistically, no doubt, Orwell also specified that what he meant by "democratic Socialism" here was "a community where people are relatively free and happy and where the main motive in life is not the pursuit of money or power." (See the reference in note 35.)

NAFTA and the Western Hemisphere

The clearest case of movement towards some potential new regional political formation outside Europe has been the North American Free Trade Agreement among Canada, the United States, and Mexico, which took effect in January 1994. Though NAFTA involves quite different arrangements than the European Union, at least a few critics have worried that it points towards an "emerging North American state."[37]

Even before the ink was dry on the three-way deal there was talk about extending it southward as well. This talk anticipated "a free-trade agreement covering most if not all of the countries of the Western Hemisphere," in "recognition that we now live in a global economy built upon three regional economies," each of which "is clustered around a dominant economy – the EC for Europe and the Middle East, the United States for North and South America, and Japan for East Asia and the Pacific."[38]

The Chile that has recently enjoyed a decade of strong economic growth is the approved candidate for a first step in this direction. Such recent Latin American regional integration schemes as the MERCOSUR trade pact among Argentina, Brazil, Paraguay, and Uruguay can be viewed as tilling still more soil for some eventual broader integration throughout the new world. A December 1994 meeting of Western Hemisphere leaders in Miami pledged to work towards a "Free Trade Agreement of the Americas" by as early as 2005.

On the other hand, NAFTA as it stands is nothing more than a trade agreement. Unlike the European Union, it is an enterprise that the mind of Adam Smith might find congenial (with the possible exception of two "side deals" on labour and the environment, inserted at the last minute to please the new Clinton administration in Washington); like the European Union, it is intended to help its partners compete more effectively in the global economy by broadening the regional base for domestic development. But NAFTA has not arisen from anything comparable to the long postwar history of the European integration movement. Its story in this sense only reaches back to the Canada-U.S. trade agreement of the late 1980s.

The Canada-U.S. agreement and the later Canada-U.S.-Mexico deal have both flowed from concerns of the Canadian and Mexican business communities over securing access to the lucrative U.S. domestic market at a time of rising pressure in the United States for protection against the global competition induced by the new economic forces. NAFTA has no common tariffs or duties on foreign goods and services from the rest of the world. Unlike in Europe, there has been no action towards or even serious talk about the eventual evolution of a single regional currency. Moreover, "the 'United States of Europe' is, as a French writer said, a creative myth. There is a strong wish for unification in political terms. That is not the case in NAFTA; there is not a political ideal of unification there."[39]

Only a year after NAFTA took effect, a cloud had obscured the future of regional integration in the Americas. Probably the most innovative (and contentious) aspect of the agreement is that it linked a low-wage, third-world (or developing) national economy with two high-wage, first-world national economies. The collapse of the Mexican peso in late 1994 and early 1995 ("the first crisis of the 21st century" on some accounts)[40] has been interpreted as a sign of the risks in innovation of this sort. Some have also gone on to read it as a sign that even as a mere trade agreement NAFTA may prove to have been a premature step in the wrong direction. Nevertheless, by the spring of 1995 political leaders in all of Canada, the United States, and Mexico were voicing continued strong support. In June 1995 official talks to bring Chile into the agreement began in Toronto.

AFTA, ASEAN, APEC, and the Asia-Pacific Region

As a sign of just how uncertain the real prospects for any particular regional *or* global, economic *or* political integration still are, there have also been voices urging that NAFTA should not confine its future expansion to the new world. In the spring of 1994 Canada's trade minister, Roy McLaren,[41] "suggested that efforts to enlarge the North American Free Trade Agreement ... should go beyond the Americas and stretch into the Asia-Pacific region."*

Prospects of this sort highlight a tension between narrower "pan-Asian" and broader "pan-Pacific" concepts of regional integration. What Europe (or the West) used to think of as the mysterious East includes both a dazzling assortment of traditional Asian cultures and the western coasts of the Americas (along with Australia and New Zealand). Japan has not been the region's only dominant first-world economy in the more recent past. Much of the initial prosperity of newly industrializing Asian countries was driven by exports into other first-world markets, especially in the U.S.A. As recently as 1989 "the United States took in $101 billion in exports from Asia-Pacific countries while Japan absorbed only $79 billion."[42]

There is a longer-term historical precedent for narrower forms of pan-Asian regional integration in what was called the "Greater East Asia Co-Prosperity Sphere" – the framework for Japan's overseas imperial expansion during the earlier twentieth century. Current Japanese "re-Asianization"

---

* Several months later Canada's prime minister, Jean Chrétien, raised the prospect of an enlargement that would stretch into the European Union as well. As noted below, by the spring of 1995 the American business press was also debating the strategic concept of a transatlantic free-trade agreement (or TAFTA), between Europe and the United States.

trends are reviving old memories of the precedent. Just before the collapse of the Bretton Woods regime in the early 1970s, one U.S. dollar was worth 360 Japanese yen; by the early spring of 1995 the dollar had (briefly) fallen just below 80 yen. Whatever the future may or may not bring, there is some hard evidence that Japan's Asia-Pacific dominance has lately been rising:

> According to an estimate by Deutsche Bank, Japan's cumulative direct investment in East Asia through 1994 totalled $64 billion, against an estimated $26 billion from the U.S. and about $7 billion from Germany. In 1993, East Asia took 36% of Japan's exports, against 17% of America's and less than 10% of Germany's or France's.[43]

The new regional institution that points most clearly towards some narrower Japanese-dominated pan-Asian integration is the ASEAN Free Trade Area (AFTA), launched in January 1993. ASEAN (the Association of South-East Asian Nations) was itself formed in 1967 – in the midst of the Vietnam War – as a political and economic alliance of Indonesia, Malaysia, the Philippines, Singapore, and Thailand. The oil-rich sultanate of Brunei joined in 1984, just after achieving its late-blooming independence from the residues of the British empire.* The rationale for AFTA in 1993 was "the recent closer economic tie-ups among the member countries and, in particular," new linkages between trade and foreign direct investment "within the region ... induced in the 1980s through the initiative of Japanese" transnational corporations.[44]

At the same time, according to Nobuo Noda of Kyoto University, if China does turn into the economic powerhouse of the twenty-first century, Japan itself will need "to keep hooked to the United States to prevent China's becoming the regional hegemon"[45] throughout the old mysterious East. Asia at large is a culturally vast and complicated place that also includes India (another culturally vast and complicated place in its own right), several important hinterlands of Islamic civilization, and for some purposes even the Russian Federation – the most logical Asian hegemon in George Orwell's original regionalist scenario of the late 1940s.

Forces of this sort point to at least some prospects of broader pan-Pacific forms of regional integration. Their clearest institutional expression is an intergovernmental forum known as Asia-Pacific Economic Co-operation

---

* By the summer of 1995, moves were afoot to bring Vietnam into ASEAN as well. And it seems that this helped prompt Washington's decision to move towards normalizing relations between Vietnam and the United States.

(APEC), established in 1989 at the instigation of Australian Prime Minister Bob Hawke. APEC's original members were the six ASEAN countries, Australia, Canada, Japan, New Zealand, South Korea, and the United States. In 1991 arrangements were made to accommodate the participation of China, Hong Kong, and Taiwan.

Mexico, Chile, and Papua New Guinea have more recently joined the forum. And in November 1994 APEC leaders committed themselves to achieving "free and open trade and investment" by 2010 for industrialized economies and 2020 for developing economies. Some six months later, however, the American business press was expressing concern that Japan's new enthusiasm for re-Asianization could undermine the goals of APEC, "which is aimed at making sure the U.S. is not kept out of an all-Asian trade bloc."[46]

By the spring of 1995 the American business press also had one eye on Asia as it pondered yet another set of regional trial balloons, this one about a potential new Transatlantic Free Trade Agreement "between like-minded, free-market, free-trade economies" in Europe and North America:

> A long-standing romance with Asia may be blinding the U.S. to the realities of Asian commerce ... The Japanese economic model is popular from Korea to Malaysia ... [A] grand Euro-American economic coalition of two continents based on free and open markets may be the only way to pressure Asians to act according to the free-trade principles from which they have benefited so much.[47]

THE LONG GATT URUGUAY ROUND AND THE NEW WORLD TRADE ORGANIZATION

Logically at least, the prospect that the United States (or NAFTA) might play a role in both the Western Hemisphere and the Asia-Pacific (or even European) regional integration movements does considerable violence to the very concept of regional integration. And with such problems in mind, as it were, at the same time that AFTA, APEC, MERCOSUR, NAFTA, and the EU were germinating during the late 1980s and early 1990s, the eighth, or Uruguay, round of the General Agreement on Tariffs and Trade was struggling to conclude a free-trade agreement for the world at large.

The GATT has its own origins in "the intensive process of postwar institution-building in the 1940s which also led to the establishment of the International Monetary Fund, the World Bank, and the United Nations itself."[48] It began in 1947 as the record of a modest conference to reduce tariffs or duties on goods crossing borders among a mere twenty-three countries. The conference was supposed to be the first project of a much more ambitious postwar creation to be known as the International Trade Organization (ITO). But in the late 1940s such a "comprehensive global trade institution" proved contentious, especially in the U.S. Congress. The ITO remained a global bureaucrats' unrealized dream.[49]

Subsequent *ad hoc* "rounds" of tariff reductions nonetheless took place under the GATT. Major reductions among sixty-two countries were achieved during the sixth (Kennedy) round between 1964 and 1967. The Kennedy Round also marked the beginning of significant participation in the negotiations by developing as well as first-world countries. The seventh (Tokyo) round, held between 1973 and 1979, involved ninety-nine countries and began to deal with so-called non-tariff as well as traditional tariff barriers to international trade.

The Uruguay Round, which began in 1986, would ultimately involve 107 countries, including every major sovereign state in the world today, except the Russian Federation and China.* (Another 28 "countries and territories" again did not participate in negotiations, but were accredited with "observer status.") With the European integration movement already under way and regional rumblings in the Americas and the Asia-Pacific region at least dimly on the horizon, it "was clear from an early date" that this "would be the most complicated of the GATT's rounds and at the same time the most critical for its future." The objective was

> not only to liberalize world trade by traditional tariff reductions and new or tighter rules on the use of non-tariff measures including barriers in new areas, but also to strengthen the system by redrafting the dispute settlement procedures and reforming the institutional basis of the GATT. A key element is the treatment of developing countries in the negotiations and the longer-term, day-to-day operations of the GATT.[50]

As more and more political reactions to the new economic forces of the 1970s and 1980s began to bump against one another in the rest of the world, the negotiators dug into their work at Geneva in Switzerland. By December 1990, just over a year after the fall of the Berlin Wall, the process had broken down. At the end of February 1991 negotiations were resumed, but they threatened to stall again at any moment.

---

* These 107 countries included the various individual members of what finally became the European Union. The EU in its own right was also a signatory to the final results of the Uruguay Round, however, and in the World Trade Organization that was eventually created by the negotiations, the EU would speak for all its 15 member states.

Finally, more than three years later, the GATT negotiators achieved a written text for a complicated new global free-trade agreement, made public at Marrakesh in Morocco on 15 April 1994 but still subject to political approval in various important places. While the involvement of both the Chinese demographic and emerging economic giant and the new Russian Federation was left dangling, the agreement covered some 80 percent of all world trade. The GATT itself was slated to be dissolved into the more formally organized World Trade Organization (WTO). The late-1940s dream of a comprehensive global trade institution was realized at last.

AT THE EDGE OF A PRECIPICE

The new WTO may prove to be a highly strategic politico-economic organization, helping to give institutional definition and shape to the world of the twenty-first century. Or it may not. We will return to the subject in the penultimate chapter of this book. For the moment, again, a few initial points of clarification are worth noting quickly.

The first is that the text of the new GATT agreement does exude much of the now characteristic late twentieth-century global spirit of free-market reform (albeit with a dense assortment of specific exceptions, phasings-in, and qualifications – particularly for developing countries). Written texts, however, can mean different things in practice, depending on exactly who brings them to life. The first big issue for the new WTO was who would be appointed as its first director. One European candidate was not "enough of a free-marketer to satisfy" even the Clinton administration in Washington. In the same U.S. eyes a South Korean prospect was from "a country whose economy is largely closed." A Dutch candidate was "popular with American business because of his adherence to free-trade economics, but some Asian nations balk at his country's colonial past."[51] In the end, both "the U.S. and Japan opposed" Renato Ruggerio from Italy, who finally won the post in the late spring of 1995.[52]

A second point is that the successive GATT rounds since the late 1940s have already done a great deal to open up and liberalize international trade. To no small extent they have served as accelerated globalizing trends in their own right. The traditional tariff as an instrument of general government policy has become increasingly obsolete (for the time being at least). As Adam Smith predicted in the late eighteenth century, this development has probably increased the wealth of at least a significant number of nations. Yet the much more extensive ambitions for a liberalized international economic order that were finally brought to life in the establishment of the WTO suggest some largely unexplored vistas of the world economy. Now that the Uruguay Round did not collapse (as so many predicted it would), some surprising new critics of these more extensive ambitions have appeared.

Christopher Farrell himself is concerned about the British "capitalist buccaneer" Sir James Goldsmith, who has been "passionately attacking global free trade and its principal institution, the General Agreement on Tariffs & Trade." Goldsmith believes that the new regime will lead to "social divisions ... deeper than anything ever envisaged by Marx." Like many others, Farrell sees Goldsmith as a throwback to "turn-of-the-century European conservative intellectuals."[53] Yet Goldsmith is not alone in his worries. Late in 1994 one of several scenarios on the ultimate effects of the new GATT agreement (constructed by the planning department at the world's largest transnational corporation, Royal Dutch Shell) was given the ominous label "Barricades." As explained by Shell planner Peter Kassler, according to this scenario,

> the General Agreement on Tariffs & Trade produces social and economic chaos. Global trade liberalization triggers unrelenting job cuts and downward pressure on wages in industrialized nations. From Kansas to Kuala Lumpur, entrenched interests team up with religious, nationalist, and other blocs to close borders. "Globalization," says Kassler, "may lead to strife among people who don't get the rewards they think they deserve."[54]

As with all the new trade agreements of the late twentieth century, it is not easy to judge just what the words on paper will induce in the real world. The new GATT round and the fledgling World Trade Organization may never be realized in ways that would achieve the ominous effects envisioned in Kassler's Barricades scenario. But there are a few senses in which they have led the global economy to the edge of a precipice. Now that we are there, even some of those who have been most vocal in urging the process along are starting to wonder whether it really does make sense to jump off.

Table 7
The GATT Negotiating Rounds, 1947–1994

Round and Dates	Place Held	No. of Countries
1. FIRST ROUND 1947	Geneva, Switzerland	23
2. ANNECY ROUND 1949	Annecy, Switzerland	13
3. TORQUAY ROUND 1951	Torquay, United Kingdom	38
4. GENEVA ROUND 1956	Geneva, Switzerland	26
5. DILLON ROUND 1960 1961	Geneva, Switzerland	26
6. KENNEDY ROUND 1964 1967	Geneva, Switzerland	62
7. TOKYO ROUND 1973 1979	Geneva, Switzerland	99
8. URUGUAY ROUND 1986 1994	Geneva, Switzerland	107

Sources: GATT; North-South Institute, Ottawa.

CHAPTER FIVE

Cultural Fallout

The High-Technological Mystique, New Migrations, and "Backlash" on Several Fronts

"The new electronic interdependence recreates the world in the image of a global village."
                                    Marshall McLuhan, 1962[1]

Along with their initial consequences for political and economic institutions, both the new economic forces of the past quarter-century and the longer evolution of the globalization process since the end of the Second World War have had broader cultural implications. It was no accident that the 1960s civil-rights movement in the United States marched vaguely in step with African decolonization. And the U.S. civil rights movement ultimately helped create Nelson Mandela's new government in South Africa – "the virtual completion of a major transformation of modern times ... the final phase in the liberation from colonialism."[2]

The third and fourth waves of the continuing industrial revolution, which have so sharply stimulated earlier globalizing trends, also continue to breed new consequences for everyday life. Many among us today can still remember the world before television, let alone fax machines, compact discs, and CD-ROM. Long-distance air travel has transformed tourism and migration. On more and more surfaces of the planet, even if you never leave the place where you live, it is becoming increasingly difficult not to be affected by emerging new forms of globalized international culture.

UNDER TECHNOLOGY'S THUMB?

In reaching for some initial handle on new cultural forms of this sort, it is easy to confuse the high technologies that have done so much to accelerate the globalization process with the more deeply rooted process itself. This seems to me a particularly awkward problem in the region of the first world where I spend most of my own time.

Especially compared with, say, Chinese culture, North American culture is still green and inexperienced. It is unusually susceptible to "technological hyperbole – systematic and unwarranted exaggeration of the anticipated general social effects of new technologies." It suffers from

> the notion that our commitment to science and technology marks a qualitative break with all previous human history, which belief beguiles us into thinking that we are now immune from the "superstitions" that ruled older civilizations. Our everyday language has become so saturated with technical jargon and scientific pronouncements that we pay too little attention to the autochthonous drives, expressed in the fear and hatred of peoples and customs different from our own, still humming deep within us.[3]

Ever since the Portuguese mariners used their Arab astrolabes to sail around the southern tip of Africa into the Indian Ocean, technology has been a key driving force in the globalization process. Continuing technological development is one important strategy for dealing with many of the cultural, political, and economic problems now emerging as a result of the dramatic acceleration of historic globalizing trends.

Especially in the first world, however, technology is not at the very bottom of the new forms of global culture that are starting to appear. The planet at large already has somewhat more than three generations of experience with the folkways of the machine civilization. It is already more than a generation since Marshall McLuhan proclaimed the electronically induced advent of the global village.

By itself, the continuing rapid pace of technological advance is introducing refinements (some of them, albeit, quite striking) rather than truly monumental changes in everyday life. As sceptics like to note, television – or for that matter radio or the motion picture or the phonograph record or even the printing press – has already built the first branches of the information highway.

The "information revolution" is a crucial key to the increasing geographic dispersal of the machine civilization in the late twentieth century. And this dispersal is having some cultural impact on the civilization itself. Fundamentally, however, it is the spread of the machine civilization the world already knows – not some new technology – that is now raising the profound challenge of a common human life on a single planet.

Microelectronic Little Brothers

Whatever the limits of their impact, some of the latest high-technological refinements in the machine civilization are certainly significant enough. And it sometimes seems that their broad cultural consequences are not what we were once led to expect.

In the late 1940s the hopelessly closed totalitarian state projected in Orwell's *Nineteen Eighty-Four* used "telescreens" to monitor even the private lives of its subjects. The most despairing message of the new communications technology was "Big Brother Is Watching You." Orwell in fact never intended to predict that the world would turn exactly in this direction. He only meant to rouse his readers' resistance to totalitarianism by exaggerating the worst prospects implicit in the experience of his own day (which had included both the undeveloped technology of television and Hitler and Stalin).

In the 1940s Orwell was obsessed by the latent horrors of the *centralizing* cultural pressures that he saw at the bottom of the globalization process. At least in the first world of the 1990s, it is often the *decentralizing* pressures of technological advance that suggest the most horrifying prospects for ordinary life. The big brothers who may or may not be watching over Western Europe, North America, and Japan today frequently appear much less troublesome than untold numbers of new microelectronic little brothers, who are acquiring twisted new technological capacities to threaten our lives. The great dictators of the twentieth century are now long dead. Their places have been taken by smaller, more obscure figures who hijack airplanes in the Mediterranean, bomb the World Trade Centre in New York, break venerable British banks overnight at branch offices in Singapore, perpetrate gas attacks on the Tokyo subway, and bomb government buildings in Oklahoma City.*

New Totalitarian Temptations

In some respects it may be true that we now have more to fear from the anarchistic than from the totalitarian cultural impulses of high technology, but in both the first and (perhaps especially) the third worlds there is a sense in which these two extremes are only opposite sides of the same troubling coin. Even in the 1990s the speed with which every new act of obscure sabotage is greeted by loud calls for more-intrusive security measures raises prospects of new big brotherhoods. The world still has more than its fair share of oppressive governments that abuse their monopolies of legitimate force.

---

* Even the not-so-great totalitarian dictators we do have today (some of whom may even be building their own nuclear bombs) seem little more than international terrorists writ large. Who, even in the West, was seriously convinced that Saddam Hussein was another Hitler?

Global economic integration under the auspices of comparatively large numbers of transnational corporations may appear less ominous than global political integration under some single world government (or even a few regional super-states), but it is nonetheless an essentially centralizing prospect. A technical report of the early 1990s has stressed that there are "frequent misconceptions" about the decentralizing biases of "the information society." The "main technological basis of the globalisation process" today is "not inherently user-friendly." It remains true that within the prevailing human institutions of technological innovation in the global village, "accessibility is dependent on organisation and so on the economic and political decisions which shape" the organizational structures of these institutions.[4]

Orwell's *Nineteen Eighty-Four* was intended as

> a show-up of the perversions to which a centralised economy is liable and which have already been partly realised in Communism and Fascism. I do not believe that the kind of society I describe necessarily *will* arrive, but ... something resembling it *could* arrive. I believe also that totalitarian ideas have taken root in the minds of intellectuals everywhere ... The scene of the book is laid in Britain in order to emphasise that the English-speaking races are not innately better than anyone else and that totalitarianism, *if not fought against*, could triumph anywhere.[5]

At the edge of the twenty-first century, it may be somewhat harder than it was in the late 1940s to see exactly how world history continues to be threatened by the perversions to which a centralized economy is liable. But what will it mean for the world's freedom to choose if the Ford Motor Company does manage to produce a single, uniform line of global cars for the entire planet? What does it mean that, after about half a century as "a loose federation of operating companies," the world's largest transnational corporation, Royal Dutch Shell, has recently moved to install "a tighter, more centralized operation, where newly appointed teams of senior executives will oversee global divisions"?[6]

Orwell's ghost is still reminding us that the perversions of centralization are problems to guard against in any version of global culture – communist, fascist, socialist, capitalist, or none of the above. In most parts of the world we have managed to get past the actual year 1984 without stumbling into the full array of fictional horrors in *Nineteen Eighty-Four*. But there is more than one road to totalitarianism. And it is no accident that young people in the global village today are still reading Orwell's last book.

MOBILITY AND MIGRATION

Dramatic improvements in communications and information technology since the end of the Second World War have been matched by almost equally dramatic improvements in older and newer technologies of transportation.

Even in the first world and even in the earlier twentieth century, the great majority of people seldom travelled vast distances. Those who migrated to the new world on sea-borne vessels typically never returned to the places of their birth. Though the exact extent of more recent trends is often exaggerated, in the very late twentieth century quite ordinary inhabitants of first-world countries can travel enormous distances on airplanes, just for vacations; the "well-educated, qualified, and rich in all countries have in general become highly mobile";[7] and people who migrate across continents on jumbo jets commonly return home for important family occasions.

In the middle of the 1990s there are apparently more than 1.3 million Filipino female workers employed as housekeepers in Italy, Japan, Canada, Saudi Arabia, Brunei, Hong Kong, Spain, the United Arab Emirates, Britain, and Singapore – supporting families back in the Philippines with the money they earn.[8] This is but one example of the new kinds of human migrations in the late twentieth century. These trends have provocative (if still quite unclear) implications for global culture.

Mass Migrations in the Earlier Globalization Process
Mass migrations have of course already played key roles in the longest-term history of globalizing trends. They began with the first waves of the modern "re-peoplings" in the Western Hemisphere, during the sixteenth and seventeenth centuries.

Today our conventional rhetoric has at least begun to recognize that European migrants did not create the new societies of the new world all by themselves. Aboriginal and even some Asian as well as many African peoples can claim credit (or even take some blame) for what "America" in all its various senses has become.

Those who worry about such things are starting to recognize as well that globalizing migrations to places other than the new world have considerable historical depth. Even the America that in some senses includes Australia and New Zealand has not been the only global emigrant destination.

According to a United Nations technical report to which I have already referred several times (and on which Christopher Farrell has also drawn in his writing), between 1870 and 1915, 36 million people left Europe, two-thirds to the United States. But the process was more widespread. Intra-continental flows were significant in Asia; on one estimate the number of Chinese and Indian emigrants – predominantly to Burma, Indonesia, Malaysia, Sri Lanka and Thailand ... exceeded European emigration ... Intra-European flows also reached significant levels, with large numbers of migrants from Austria, Hungary and Italy seeking ... work in France, Germany and Switzerland.[9]

The New Migrations of the Late Twentieth Century
This historical background casts the new globalizing migration patterns of the late twentieth century in a somewhat less unfamiliar light than they sometimes appear at first blush. However, for better or worse, it is historically true that the cultural mainstream in the United States (for instance) has been dominated by people of European descent. From the standpoint of this cultural mainstream, in the United States and in several related first-world countries, international migrations since the late 1960s point to some dramatic new vistas of cultural diversity.

Diversity of this sort is far from a new phenomenon in world history. India, with sixteen languages, four major religions, and three main racial groups, has been an unusually diverse place for centuries. Even before the 1870–1913 era of accelerated globalizing trends, Indian and Chinese migrants had a long history in the regions of the Indian and Pacific oceans.

Though "Malays" form a clear majority in Malaysia today, the country has an Indian minority that is almost as significant comparatively as African-Americans in the United States, and a Chinese community with more relative demographic weight than the present French-speaking population in Canada. South Africa has substantial Asian and European minorities as well as an African majority. Brazil has a Portuguese/African/"mulatto" majority, and Italian, German, Japanese, Indian, Jewish, and Arab minorities.

The new international migration patterns of the late twentieth century nonetheless do have two novel features. The first turns around some striking changes in some parts of Western Europe and (much more strikingly) in North America and Australia. During the four decades that preceded the American Civil War (and after the legal importation of African slaves had ended in 1808), 95 percent of all legal immigrants to the United States came from north and west Europe. During the first two decades of the twentieth century 41 percent came from north and west Europe, and 44 percent from south and east Europe. During the first half of the 1980s only 12 percent came from all parts of Europe, while 36 percent came from Latin America, and 47 percent from Asia.[10]

Throughout the nineteenth century the overwhelming majority of migrants to the new British colonial societies in Canada, Australia, and New Zealand came from the United Kingdom (and in the case of English-speaking migrants to the old French colony of Canada, initially from the United States). During the twentieth century increasingly larger numbers came from other parts of Europe, but by the late 1980s the top-ten source countries for migrants to Australia were the United Kingdom, New Zealand, Vietnam, the Philippines, South Africa, Malaysia, China, Hong Kong, Lebanon, and Sri Lanka.[11] The parallel top-ten places for migrants to Canada were Hong Kong, Poland, the Philippines, Vietnam, India, the United Kingdom, Portugal, the United States, Lebanon, and China.[12] Even in the United Kingdom of the late 1980s some 4.5 percent of the population was taken up by Indian, West Indian, Pakistani, and other minority "ethnic" groups.[13] Other parts of Western Europe had "also received developing-country migrants, who make up small but visible minorities."[14]

Cultural Diversity and the New Global Middle Class
The second novel feature of these trends is that – no doubt not altogether accidentally – they have coincided with the more recent globalizing expansion of European and especially North American (and perhaps even more especially Anglo-American) transnational corporations.

To some significant extent, the new culturally diverse mass migrations to the non-Japanese first world of the late twentieth century are mixed in with Cyrus Freidheim's global corporation, whose "executives are citizens of the world" and "play no favorites." These migrations are particular regional reflections of Christopher Farrell's point that late twentieth-century global "capitalism is triumphant because it is multicultural." And they highlight the practical social meaning of the argument that "you can't have globalization of economics without globalization of culture."

The most provocative logical implication is that the recent dramatically accelerated globalization of economics, as it were, has begun to spawn some new and even historically unique global culture – a kind of universal composite of all the diverse regional cultures that have marked world history down to the present moment of great transformation.

One (perhaps) increasingly influential vision of the future has it that the key vehicle for the diffusion of this culture will be Farrell's new, highly mobile "global middle class," which (as the Stanford sociology professor John Meyer has put it) shares "similar concepts of citizenship, similar ideas about economic progress, and a similar picture of human rights." According to U.S. business writer Robert J. Dowling, the vision assumes "a 21st century economy so networked and borderless that skilled, highly trained professionals from many nations will create a new international class."[15]

This vision points to what could become an unusually potent brand of twenty-first-century globalization ideology. One mark of the ideology's potency is the extent to which it logically unites two prominent factions in recent political and cultural debate (in key parts of the first world at least) – progressive right-wing apostles of global capitalism and free-market reform, and progressive left-wing apostles of political correctness and cultural inclusion.

In the U.S.A. today, for instance, business writer Christopher Farrell and Edward Said (the Arab-American literary critic who, as noted earlier in this book, has written so astutely about the agonizing old imperial cultural origins of today's globalizing trends) likely disagree on a host of specific current issues. They both believe, however, that the future belongs to culturally diverse societies linked by a borderless ethos that has "consolidated the mixture of cultures and identities on a global scale," and in which no one is "purely *one* thing."[16]

The Real Prospects for a Diverse Global Culture

With such other current phenomena as "ethnic cleansing" staining the late twentieth-century air, it is obvious that, like Cyrus Freidheim's global corporation, the concept of a universal diverse global culture is still much more of an ideal than a reality. Yet it is impossible to live in the kind of North American city I inhabit myself without sensing that, in some places, some type of new culturally diverse society has begun to put down a few authentic roots.

In Canada in 1981 "the foreign born represented 16 percent of the total population compared to 21 percent in Australia and 6 percent in the United States."[17] By 1991 this proportion had increased to just under 23 percent in Australia and 8 percent in the United States (compared with some 6 percent in Sweden, 9 percent in Belgium, and 17 percent in Switzerland).[18] The "foreign born," or as the official statistics now put it, the "immigrant population," was still 16 percent of the total in Canada in 1991, but in the most populous Canadian province of Ontario it was just under 24 percent. In Ontario's capital city of Toronto – in the old city proper where Marshall McLuhan was living when he coined the phrase "global village" in the 1960s – the 1991 immigrant population was 44 percent of the total population. In the two adjacent suburban cities of York and North York it was as high as 50 percent.

Some 26 percent of the 1991 population in the city of Toronto reported various combinations of "multiple ethnic origins." Among the remainder reporting single origins, 17 percent claimed to be British, 8 percent Chinese,

8 percent Portuguese, 5 percent Canadian,* 5 percent Italian, 3 percent Jewish, 2 percent Black, 2 percent Polish, 2 percent German, 2 percent Filipino, 2 percent Greek, 2 percent French, 1 percent East Indian, 1 percent Ukrainian, 1 percent Spanish, 1 percent Dutch, 1 percent Hungarian, and 1 percent Vietnamese. Another 10 percent reported one of close to ninety other single origins.[19]

It is true enough that, even in those places where this kind of cultural diversity has taken root, its ultimate future remains anxiously unknown. The recent grim history of the former Yugoslavia – once widely thought to be a progressive model of an ethnically pluralistic nation-state – is only one small piece of evidence against rosily optimistic speculations.

Moreover, when Edward Said tries to reassure those who find his cultural criticism alarming, he confines his rhetoric to the most obvious specific geography:

> Despite its extraordinary cultural diversity, the United States is, and will surely remain, a coherent nation. The same is true of other English-speaking countries (Britain, New Zealand, Australia, Canada) and even of France, which now contains large groups of immigrants.[20]

Even if these places do listen to the likes of both Edward Said and Christopher Farrell and successfully incubate highly diverse but nonetheless coherent new global populations, all too many stubborn facts suggest that this is an unlikely pattern for the planet at large.

The 1980s brought a "sudden influx of cheap foreign (Asian) labour" even to Japan, but this only prompted the isolationist Japanese intellectual Nishio Kanji to reflect on how "our great advantage has always been the homogeneity of our race ... that is the great source of our strength."[21] China is more culturally diverse than it may seem at first glance (only somewhat more than 70 percent of its almost 1.2 billion people speak the dominant Mandarin language), but it is notably more homogeneous than India. Though Malaysia is a diverse place in some ways, in the middle of the 1990s its government "talks of building an Asian economic bloc excluding the U.S., Australia, and New Zealand – a 'caucus without caucasians.'" Some new proponents of closer economic ties between North America and the European Union "seem intent on creating a 'caucus with only caucasians.'"[22]

---

* "Canadian" (like "American" or "Australian" for that matter) is still not treated as an official "ethnic origin" category by government statisticians, but in the 1991 census some respondents volunteered their origin as Canadian in an open-ended category on the official forms.

In the end, the late twentieth-century prominence of cultural diversity in Edward Said's "United States ... Britain, New Zealand, Australia, Canada ... and even ... France" may turn out to be merely an ironic, geographically specific, and limited last legacy of the old sea-borne empires of Europe. The British empire, for instance, bequeathed an almost dazzling new kind of ethnically diverse English-language culture with some authentic global reach. Perhaps the most interesting English literature of the later twentieth century has been created by such colourful authors as Chinua Achebe, V.S. Naipaul, R.K. Narayan, and Derek Walcott.

If you are connected to the right branch of the televised information highway, you can commune with this particular borderless culture every night on the BBC World News. For large enough numbers of the almost half-billion people in the world who do speak English, this culture can be a fascinating "place." It has much of the cosmopolitan attraction of the old empire on which the sun never set – cleansed of at least some of the empire's worst features, and it does have a few universal overtones. However, it is a vast distance away from any altogether universal diverse global culture. It is still in many ways merely the culture of the old British empire, wearing some fresh make-up and dressed in the latest clothes.

With a somewhat different twist, there are those who argue that the most authentic regional history of North America is in fact a history of cultural diversity. While in a few senses it is true that "fundamentally the civilization of North America is the civilization of Europe,"[23] the African contribution to "America" – from jazz to the successor pop musics that now circle the globe – has been fundamental too. As some see it (and I should note that I find this argument attractive), the highest destiny of the new world is to blend all the cultures of the African, Asian, and European old worlds. We who choose to live in North America today also choose to be the descendants of the Iroquois, the Cherokee, the Sioux, the Apache, the Maya, and the Cree. The deepest roots of the North American future lie in the cross-cultural, Indian-European, frontier middle ground of the sixteenth, seventeenth, and eighteenth centuries, between "the other" and "us."[24]

In the age of the multinational corporation, this new version of a longstanding American universalism – if that is what it is – has its own degrees of global reach. You can now buy McDonald's hamburgers in seventy-nine countries of the world (and in the last half of the 1990s, "having all but saturated America, the company is opening two foreign stores for every new U.S. outlet").[25] If your television is suitably connected, again, you can commune with the American revolutionary variation on the globalizing English-language universe every night, on the CNN World News. Yet, this pervasive American globalizing culture, too, is far from being a universal diverse global culture. Its weakness as well as its strength is that it still has so much of the raw naivety of youth.

CULTURAL "BACKLASH" – ON SEVERAL FRONTS

Another weakness of the late twentieth-century Anglo-American globalization ideology that the likes of Farrell and Said are urging upon at least some branches of today's humanity is that its domestic support in the United States itself is shaky at best. In the spring of 1995 the U.S. presidential contender Patrick Buchanan made some remarks to help launch an event known as Immigration Awareness Week – "a campaign by anti-immigrant groups to close America's borders to newcomers." As a result of neighbouring Canada's two official languages and official multiculturalism policy, Buchanan declared, the place was "coming apart," and "I don't want that to happen to our country." He went on to applaud a recent book called *Alien Nation*, which argues that "the United States is risking its sovereignty and straining its social fabric by allowing in too many non-European immigrants."[26]

It still seems unlikely that Patrick Buchanan or anyone like him could ever become president of the United States (or that the vaguely analogous Jean-Marie Le Pen could ever be president of France). But Buchanan is articulating only one of several increasingly visible species of backlash against emerging forms of globalized international culture – in many parts of the world. Monumental changes and great transformations in world history can also provoke monumental resistance. As the last decade of the twentieth century has progressed, cultural backlash against the dramatically accelerated globalization process has often seemed on the verge of becoming stronger than the process itself.

It can easily be said that this backlash is not rational, and it is often surrounded by deep confusion. The U.S. private militia groups that surfaced in the mass media after the April 1995 bombing in Oklahoma City, for instance, are ardent supporters of "limited government." Some apparently believe that the United Nations is about to invade the United States and "replace U.S. democracy with one world government."[27] It is not, however, government that represents the emerging new forms of global culture against which the private militia groups are organizing. It is private multinational or transnational corporations. These corporations support limited government as well. In the midst of their confusion the private militia groups are aiding and abetting the globalizing trends they mean to oppose.*

---

* Though on the not entirely implausible argument that the present federal government in Washington (regardless of its partisan complexion) does a better job of representing the interests of U.S.-based multinational corporations than it does those of its domestic electorate, the private militia groups may not be quite as confused as they appear at first glance.

Cultural backlash against recent accelerated globalizing trends is of course not at all confined to the United States, or France, or any other part of the first world. Speaking metaphorically, the machine civilization *is* what everyone wants in the end. But from the start of the first industrial revolution in Britain well over 200 years ago now, technological advance has regularly provoked its own monumental forms of more (and less) transient protest.

The Ayatollah Khomeni and his successors in Iran would probably agree with George Orwell's pronouncement that "all sensitive people are revolted by industrialism and its products." Despite the historic Islamic incubation of the Portuguese globalization pioneers, increasingly global brands of Islamic fundamentalism tend to see the late twentieth-century machine civilization as a bearer of the secularist (and even evil) values of American universalism – or Western culture. As Christopher Farrell observes (and as already noted at the start of this book), "policymakers worldwide" are increasingly concerned that "rising social and economic pressures in a competitive global economy will spark 'culture wars.' Hinduism vs. Islam. Confucian values vs. Western values."[28]

In the midst of these rising social and economic pressures, some forms of cultural backlash against globalizing trends are in fact rational enough. And even in its most confused expressions backlash can usually be traced back to some approximation of common sense. What the technology theorist William Leiss has urged about technological change also applies to the deeper globalization process at large:

> For those experiencing some negative effects from new technologies ... it is small consolation to be told that there is a clear net social benefit ... [I]t is perfectly "sensible" for those who believe ... that they might be disadvantaged to oppose such developments, if they can, or at least to delay their implementation until someone offers them reasonable compensation. Those who attack new technologies are often called "Luddites," a label that stands for irrational and futile opposition to progress. Such a stance may very well be futile, but it is by no means irrational.[29]

From another angle again, some now argue that the most influential changes in the increasingly globalized culture of the future could include the biotechnology of gene management, which "may allow us to preempt many diseases and dramatically manage population growth, fundamentally altering social trends."[30] There is troubling evidence, however, that at least some related forms of biotechnology are themselves breeding species of cultural backlash that go beyond the conscious wills of human beings. In the particular case of infectious bacteria, some biotechnologists have lately been more impressed by the current problems of "re-emerging old diseases" than by the future potential for altering social trends and pre-empting disease through gene management. Historically,

> antibiotics have been used in a manner unintentionally calculated to maximize the evolutionary selection for antibiotic resistance in the bacteria – and that is exactly what has been achieved ... Since the well-publicized appearance of tuberculosis strains resistant to multiple antibiotics, it has become almost orthodox to prophesy the end of the antibiotic era.[31]

And, in language that points to the more general roots of the particular horrors raised by the biological scourge of AIDS:

> Our immune system evolved under the pressure developing species felt from the world of micro-organisms, many of which were capable of killing them. Over the millennia, an adaptive struggle has gone on occurring relentlessly as organisms that wish to survive and perpetuate their "selfish genes" encounter ever more sophisticated immunological weaponry. Just a quick glance at the scorecard for 1994, however, would see any fair judge putting the germ world ahead on points.[32]

THE MYSTERIOUS WORLD OF THE FUTURE TODAY

The most balanced context for assessing all forms of cultural backlash against today's imminent great transformation in world history is the longest term. In this context "our" planet has been moving inexorably towards some new form of global culture ever since Bartholomew Diaz doubled the Cape of Good Hope and launched the long human process of discovering the full extent of the world. We have now reached a point in this process where, even if we ourselves see only a small fraction of this world face to face, we have learned too much about it to imagine or feel or believe in anything less than some comprehensive global framework.

Many thoughtful people have grasped the significance of this great transformation for much of the twentieth century – especially since the end of the Second World War. (Both European Marxism and liberalism in the later nineteenth century also reflected culturally warped Eurocentric apprehensions of what lay ahead.) The Anglo-American poet T.S. Eliot was born in St. Louis, Missouri, in 1888 and died in London, England, in 1965. In the

1980s it was aptly enough said that his writing "represents the brilliant efflorescence of a dying culture."[33] In 1946, however, he had explained to a German radio audience that "one unity of culture is that of the people who live together and speak the same language ... But the cultures of different peoples do affect each other: in the world of the future it looks as if every part of the world would affect every other part."[34]

Who can seriously doubt that this world of the future has now unmistakably arrived? Personally, I think there are good as well as bad reasons for many different forms of cultural backlash against the historic globalizing trends of today. But I also think we really have begun to create some new form of global culture, and it strikes me as a great and progressive, as well as an inescapable, adventure.

Just where this adventure will lead us is a mystery. Whatever shape the new global culture may finally take, it will only be convincing if it relates to the ordinary life of everyone on the planet. This would involve a stupendous transformation that we have only just begun to think about. The narrow globalization ideology of some rising "new international class" may or may not play a useful role in getting us from here to there. But it cannot be the new global culture itself. If this international class were to get us anywhere at all, it would have to grow beyond both the eighteenth-century liberal ideas of the Anglo-American bourgeoisie and the (in the end) equally narrow rhetoric of cultural inclusion in the "United States ... Britain, New Zealand, Australia, Canada ... and even ... France."

Table 8
Cultural Diversity in North America, 1991
(% Population by Ethnic Origin in Canada's Three Largest Census Metropolitan Areas)

Ethnic Origin	Montreal	Toronto	Vancouver
MULTIPLE ORIGINS	11.7	24.3	35.4
SINGLE ORIGINS			
Aboriginal	0.4	0.2	0.8
British	5.4	19.3	23.1
Canadian	0.3	6.9	1.5
French	59.0	1.3	1.8
Dutch	0.1	0.8	1.6
German	0.6	1.8	3.9
Greek	1.6	1.6	0.4
Hungarian	0.2	0.6	0.5
Italian	5.3	8.1	1.9
Jewish	2.5	3.0	0.7
Polish	0.6	1.9	0.9
Portuguese	1.0	3.2	0.6
Spanish	0.6	0.9	0.3
Ukrainian	0.3	1.1	1.5
Arab	1.8	0.7	0.2
Black	1.2	3.3	0.3
Caribbean	0.8	1.3	0.1
Chinese	1.1	6.0	10.6
East Indian	0.5	3.7	4.2
Filipino	0.3	1.7	1.6
Korean	0.1	0.6	0.5
Latin American	0.8	0.7	0.4
Vietnamese	0.6	0.6	0.6
West Asian	0.7	0.9	0.5
Other	2.5	5.5	6.1

Source: Statistics Canada.

CHAPTER SIX

TILTING AT WINDMILLS

THE QUEST FOR GLOBAL GOVERNANCE IN THE TWENTIETH CENTURY

"There must be, not a balance of power, but a community of power; not organized rivalries, but an organized common peace."

Woodrow Wilson, 1917[1]

The increasing intensity of cultural backlash against late twentieth-century globalizing trends has something to do with the current revival of interest in (as the most up-to-date English usage has it) "global governance." Like Christopher Farrell and many others, those active in this cause stress that "we are at the threshold of a new era" in world history, whose "newness is self-evident; people everywhere know it."[2] Global governance advocates, however, have less faith in the capacity of the liberal ideas of the bourgeoisie to rise all the way to the challenges of the new era, even when these ideas are "coupled with the spread of technological innovations."[3]

These advocates are the heirs to an international political tradition that stretches back to the end of the First World War – or even to the earlier 1870–1913 era of accelerated globalization (which the First World War and its aftermath helped to stifle and repress). It is small-minded to belittle either this historic movement or its current institutional base in the various organizations of the United Nations. For certain purposes even aggressively philistine apostles of Adam Smith pay lip service to the tradition's characteristic "values of internationalism, the primacy of the rule of law world-wide, and institutional reforms that secure and sustain them."[4] However, the past 100 years have not been at all kind to these values. And it still takes monumental degrees of faith to believe that the foreseeable future will prove significantly more hospitable.

GLOBAL GOVERNANCE AND GLOBAL SECURITY

The overriding historic objective of both the United Nations, established at the end of the Second World War, and its predecessor organization, the League of Nations (established at the end of the First World War), was to prevent appallingly destructive "world wars." As Samuel Eliot Morison observed, the Seven Years' War of the mid-eighteenth century was really the first world war. The long-term globalization process has recurrently spawned such monumental conflicts, and as the technology of the industrial revolution advanced, these conflicts reached new heights of irrational destruction in what we do call the First World War today. Because there actually was a second world war after the League of Nations had been formed in the wake of the first one, the League had clearly failed in meeting its overriding objective. On the same logic, because we have not yet had a third world war, the United Nations has at least been less of a failure than its predecessor.

Virtually all analysts of the international system, on the other hand, would agree that the United Nations itself has played only a limited part in preventing a third world war. The key here has been that no leaders of a major nuclear power have so far been quite so egotistically foolish as to risk the now supremely monumental destruction that such a conflict would almost certainly entail. As Orwell speculated in the late 1940s, "the fear inspired by the atomic bomb and other weapons yet to come" has been "so great that everyone" (after Hiroshima and Nagasaki) has refrained "from using them."[5]

Anyone alive at the time of the 1961 Cuban missile crisis can remember that the balance of nuclear terror did not always appear so benign. In the late twentieth century, though, it often seems that here again there is more to fear from little brothers than from big ones. The proliferation of nuclear weapons among minor powers is frequently pictured as a leading current issue of global security. A key recommendation of an intriguing international non-governmental organization (NGO) known as the Commission on Global Governance (which published a detailed report in 1995) is "the indefinite extension of the Non-Proliferation Treaty,"[6] first negotiated in 1968 and recurrently expanded since then.

There was nonetheless some almost serious war-mongering talk in Western Europe and North America during the early 1980s, when the deepest implications of the new economic forces of the late twentieth century first began to set in. Jimmy Carter's last State of the Union message in 1980, for instance, warned that the United States was prepared to go to war to protect oil-supply routes in the Persian Gulf. In 1981 Ronald Reagan began a series of sharp increases in U.S. defence spending and ordered the production of neutron bombs. In 1982 Reagan urged Margaret Thatcher's Britain to join the United States in a worldwide "crusade for freedom," and in March 1983 he delivered his "evil empire" indictment of the Soviet Union. A month later François Mitterand's government expelled forty-seven Soviet diplomats and other citizens from France. Though there has mercifully been no third world war since 1945, there have been many smaller wars, including the United State's war in Vietnam, the Soviet Union's war in Afghanistan, and the United Kingdom's war against Argentina over the Falkland Islands.

On the eve of the fiftieth anniversary of VE-Day in 1995, the Euro-British writer Timothy Garton Ash even raised the prospect of a major military conflagration yet again in Europe, where a small war was "actually being waged ... bloodily and brutally and – with almost too crude an irony – in a place called Sarajevo" (where the First World War had also begun, in the now long-ago summer of 1914):

> All divisions of time are artificial, and perhaps the last five years of the twentieth century and the second millennium AD should be considered no differently from any other five years. But the millennial deadline does concentrate the mind. In these next five years we probably have a larger chance but also a larger danger than at any time in the past fifty. The chance is that in the year 2000 more of Europe will be more peaceful, prosperous, democratic and free than ever before in its history. The danger can also be simply described. If we get things wrong now then some time in the early part of the next century we will stop talking about May 8 as the end of *the* war in Europe – because there'll be another.[7]

THE EXPANDING AGENDA OF GLOBAL GOVERNANCE

Reducing the threat of monumentally destructive global warfare remains the overriding objective of the global governance movement. According to article 1 of the United Nations Charter, the "primary purpose of the UN is, 'To maintain international peace ... and to that end to take effective collective measures.'"[8]

The dramatically accelerated globalizing trends of the late twentieth century, however, have also raised aspirations to a wider global governance agenda. And the end of the Cold War has raised hopes that both the United Nations' traditional primary purpose and its wider aspirations (along with those of an array of cognate international organizations) can be more effectively realized than in the past.

On this view, during its first half-century the UN has been only slightly less of a failure than the earlier League of Nations "because the most powerful nations were, until recently, locked in the frozen embrace of the Cold

War."⁹ Now that this embrace has thawed, there ought to be room for larger global political ambitions.

In a general way, the objects of these ambitions are no less than the problems of the globalization process itself. The crux of the argument has been summarized in the Commission on Global Governance's recent report:

> The term globalization has been used primarily to describe some key aspects of world economic activity. But several other, less benign, activities, including the drug trade, terrorism, and traffic in nuclear materials have also been globalized ...
>
> Technological advances have made national frontiers more porous. States retain sovereignty, but governments have suffered an erosion in their authority ...
>
> The links among poverty, population, consumption, and environment and the systemic nature of their interactions have become clearer. So has the need for integrated global approaches to their management.[10]

Three more-specific broad-issue areas illustrate the practical scope of the agenda for "integrated global ... management." The first involves the overarching goal of "strengthening the rule of law world-wide." For strong advocates of this goal, the historic globalization process has now evolved to the point where not just major world wars, but all warfare and violent conflict generally, have become obsolete means of legitimately resolving human disputes. The world at large has reached a stage of political development vaguely comparable to that reached by local states in an earlier era.

The view is not at all new. A U.S. delegation brought a proposal for an international court of justice to the so-called first Hague Conference of 1899. The globalization process today, however, is much more advanced than it was a century ago. According to the Commission on Global Governance: "The global neighbourhood of the future must be characterized by law and the reality that all, including the weakest, are equal under the law and none, including the strongest, is above it."[11]

Another broad-issue area is global ecology and the global environment. This does have long-term roots in the critique of the industrial revolution popularly dramatized by the British Luddites in the early nineteenth century, but the crux of the issue today can be more scientifically conceived as a massive biological backlash against late twentieth-century globalization. Its most apocalyptic articulations began to surface in the early 1970s:

The explosive growth of the human population is the most significant terrestrial event of the past million millennia ... Mankind itself may stand on the brink of extinction ... Spaceship Earth is now filled to capacity or beyond ... The food-producing mechanism is being sabotaged. The devices that maintain the atmosphere are being turned off. The temperature-control system is being altered at random. Thermonuclear bombs, poison gases, and super-germs have been manufactured ... In the past few years some people have begun to face the immensity of the spaceship's peril and have begun to grope for ways of avoiding catastrophe.[12]

Almost twenty-five years after these particular words were written, the spaceship is somehow still intact, but more-measured concerns about its long-term ecological future have remained influential. In 1991 the World Bank and two UN agencies launched a $1.2-billion "3-year pilot programme" known as the Global Environment Facility, "to assist developing countries in their efforts to protect the global environment in four focal areas: global warming, pollution of international waters, loss of biodiversity and depletion of the ozone layer."[13]

A third broad-issue area involves the higher management of the world economy itself. The most ardent disciples of Adam Smith would argue that not very much management of this sort is required. For varying reasons, varying advocates of global governance would disagree.

The aspirations of the United Nations in this context are shared by a number of related international organizations. They include the World Bank and the International Monetary Fund – created by the same Bretton Woods conference that spawned the global financial stabilization system that was abandoned in 1971. They also include the present Group of Seven countries, whose various regular meetings constitute the closest approximation of a higher management for the global economy now at hand, and the new World Trade Organization (spawned by the ultimately successful Uruguay Round of the General Agreement on Tariffs and Trade).

THE LESSONS OF THE PAST

Any culture with even a qualified faith in technology will look sceptically at the proposition that nothing that has not already happened in the past can happen in the future. Even an institution of mere governance, on the other hand, "is not a machine but a living thing."[14] The pasts of such things do tend to condition their futures. And the living evolution of the global governance movement since the late nineteenth century can help illuminate the prospects for both its traditional and wider agendas today.

This evolution is often traced back to the two Hague conferences of

1899 and 1907 (both held in the Netherlands city of the same name). The key item on the agenda of the first conference was disarmament. The gathering brought together twenty-seven different countries at the instigation of the czar of Russia. Though the Hague conferences showed some foresight about the most destructive tendencies of the 1870–1913 globalization era, they did not prevent the First World War. Even so, they were later regarded as a precedent of sorts for the establishment of the League of Nations in 1919.[15]

The League was headquartered at Geneva in Switzerland. All told, sixty-three national states were members at one point or another ("nearly all the sovereign states of the globe"[16] at the time), but only thirty-one remained with the organization from its formal beginning in 1920 to its formal disbanding in 1946. Thanks to the Senate in Washington, the United States was never a member. Japan was a member only from 1920 to 1935, Germany from 1926 to 1935, and the U.S.S.R. from 1934 to 1939. Another weakness was that the "League's machinery for enforcing its decisions ... depended on a unanimous vote of the Assembly,"[17] in which each member state had one ballot. Even before the Second World War broke out in the late summer of 1939, the League's powerlessness to prevent Japan's occupation of Manchuria in 1931 and Italy's invasion of Ethiopia in 1935 was widely regarded as the final proof of its failure.

The United Nations was founded on 26 June 1945, just over two months before the end of the Second World War in the Pacific. It is still headquartered in New York City today. It had fifty-one member states when it began in 1945, 76 in 1955, 118 in 1965, 143 in 1975, 158 in 1985, and 185 in 1995. There is now no major national state in the world that does not belong to the organization.

One mark of institutional continuity between the UN and the earlier League is that the head of both organizations has been called "secretary general." In an effort to avoid the weaknesses of the League Assembly, however, "primary responsibility for the maintenance of international peace" was given to the UN Security Council, which included permanent representation from the U.S.A., the U.S.S.R., Britain, France, and China. Alas (on Joseph Stalin's insistence), each permanent council member also had a veto. As the frozen embrace of the Cold War set in, the U.S.S.R.* began to cast "its veto not

---

* There was an intriguing change in most-frequent-veto-user status as time went on: "In the first 28 years of the United Nations, the Soviet Union vetoed 104 Security Council resolutions, while the United States vetoed none. In the next 16 years, however, a very different picture emerged. The Soviet Union vetoed only 10 Security Council resolutions, while the United States vetoed 42." (Anatol and Anthony Rapoport, *Canada and the World: An Agenda for the Last Decade of the Millennium* [Toronto: Science for Peace/Samuel Stevens, 1992], 87.)

merely in exceptional cases, as the Charter had anticipated, but almost as a matter of routine."[18]

The story of global governance since the Hague conferences has a number of broad features that can help illuminate the future. To start with, like the globalization process itself, the beginnings of global governance have some pronounced Eurocentric features. The very concept of a "league of nations" had grown out of the evolution of the European system of sovereign states – customarily said to have begun with the Treaty of Westphalia, which ended the Thirty Years' War in 1648.[19] Part of the global managerial regime the League tried to launch in 1920 was already being handled by the "colonial governance structures" of the European empires, during the penultimate chapters in the story of "the enforced liberalism of the colonial era."[20] There were a few mild acknowledgments of this awkward fact in the League's "Covenant."[21] It is only in the last few decades of the twentieth century that the quest for an authentically global political order (as now expressed in the United Nations) has begun to transcend its European imperial origins.

Another intriguing point involves the ambivalent role of the United States – the, in some respects, first decolonized nation. Despite the ultimate U.S. absence from the League of Nations, the organization was to no small extent the brainchild of the U.S. president of the day, Woodrow Wilson. It reflected a particular American universalist grasp of the European, or Western, destiny. Wilson's failure to convince the U.S. Senate to approve American participation in the League literally paralyzed him for a time and led to his death at the age of sixty-seven in 1924.[22] The overwhelming global economic dominance of the United States at the end of the Second World War was enough to let American universalist impulses triumph over American isolationist instincts in the formation of the United Nations. But there is some evidence that the more recent inevitable decline in this dominance could swing pendulums in opposite directions once again. Like others in the U.S.A. today, the "73 freshmen House Republicans" elected to Congress in 1994 are wary of international organizations and "one-world government."[23]

In a fundamental sense, it is worth recalling that government (or the state) at any level finally means "a human community that (successfully) claims the *monopoly of the legitimate use of physical force* within a given territory."[24] A truly effective global political order would be one that transferred at least some of this monopoly, as currently exercised by national states, to an institution that speaks for the territory of the world at large. During the debates on the formation of the League of Nations in 1919, the French Radical party politician Léon Bourgeois advanced a proposal for a permanent "international force" that could overcome armed opposition to the League's decisions.25 The proposal was never acted on, partly because of practical political difficulties that have been regularly (if sadly) acknowledged in virtually all subsequent debate on the subject. Yet the historic failure to create Bourgeois's international force owed a great deal as well to some profound philosophical and moral concerns. And, like it or not, they are with us still.

SOME PROBLEMS OF UNITED NATIONS REFORM

About a dozen years after the end of the Second World War the (Jewish) German-American political philosopher Hannah Arendt eloquently spelled out one version of these concerns:

> No matter what form a world government with centralized power over the whole globe might assume, the very notion of one sovereign force ruling the whole earth, holding the monopoly of all means of violence, unchecked and uncontrolled by other sovereign powers, is not only a forbidding nightmare of tyranny, it would be the end of all political life as we know it.26

No doubt with such thoughts at the back of their minds, the authors of the 1995 report of the Commission on Global Governance have taken pains to stress that

> global governance is not global government. No misunderstanding should arise from the similarity of the terms. We are not proposing movement towards world government, for were we to travel in that direction we could find ourselves in an even less democratic world than we have – one more accommodating to power, more hospitable to hegemonic ambition, and more reinforcing of the roles of states and governments rather than the rights of people.27

From one angle, these are certainly the right things to say. However, insofar as ideas of this sort are meant to be taken altogether seriously, they betray some fundamental limitations of global governance as a comprehensive approach to addressing the problems of globalization.

As the concept's most ardent advocates themselves acknowledge, there is an important sense in which Léon Bourgeois was right in 1919. According to one of many like-minded late twentieth-century commentators: "If the United Nations is to fulfil its mission as set forth in the *Preamble* and *Chapter 1* of its *Charter*, it will have to be thoroughly reformed. Its first priority should be the formation of an effective and viable Peace Force."28 The Commission on Global Governance itself finally recommends:

The UN needs to be able to deploy credible and effective peace enforcement units at an early stage in a crisis and at short notice. It is high time that a UN Volunteer Force was established. We envisage a force with a maximum of 10,000 personnel. It would not take the place of ... traditional peace-keeping forces ... Rather, it would give the Security Council the ability to back up preventive diplomacy with a measure of immediate and convincing deployment on the ground.[29]

A force of this sort, no doubt, is not at all comparable to Hannah Arendt's "one sovereign force ruling the whole earth, holding the monopoly of all means of violence, unchecked and uncontrolled by other sovereign powers." Many ordinary citizens of the world would likely agree that some high-minded international force ought to be trying to keep the peace worldwide. And of course the great practical stumbling block is simply "the resistance of the powerful to change."[30] On the other hand, other ordinary citizens are also entitled to wonder whether establishing even a modest UN volunteer force would amount to a first step down a slippery slope to something much more ominous. In one sense, it is easy enough to agree with a related proposition advanced by the Commission on Global Governance: "Military force is not a legitimate political instrument except in self-defence or under UN auspices."[31] In another sense, accepting this proposition does imply some degree of movement towards world government and not mere global governance.

These considerations raise extremely difficult questions that quite likely cannot be resolved at all quickly – if at all – even now that the Cold War is over. (Would you or I, for instance, accept that the current UN secretary general, Boutros Boutros-Ghali, has the moral authority or legitimacy to order the use of armed force against our country if he believes our country has committed some offence against the international community? If he does not, who or what does have this kind of authority? Is it the UN Security Council, which currently includes a permanent representative of the national government that ordered the crushing of largely unarmed protesters in Beijing on 4 June 1989? If any international leader or institution is conceded this authority, what is to protect the rest of us from its potential usurpation by a global tyrant?) It may very well be that "because the changes required are so profound ... one will have to wait for action until cataclysmic crisis conditions occur."[32]

Meanwhile, even to grow and develop as a useful and important vehicle for more limited forms of global political activity, the late twentieth-century United Nations stands in need of major reform. Above all else, reform of the Security Council is pressing for two reasons: first, its permanent membership no longer reflects the reality of global power; secondly, its credibility as an impartial intervenor in situations that threaten common security is undermined by the disproportionate influence within it of Northern, and especially North Atlantic states.[33]

A variety of specific proposals have lately been advanced. With an eye on such recent developments as the European Union, NAFTA, MERCOSUR, and AFTA, a North American study group has urged that the council "represent continental or subcontinental regions, rather than selected and elected particular states as at present."[34] The Commission on Global Governance has envisioned a phased process of Security Council reform taking place over some two decades and starting with "a new class of five 'standing' members ... selected by the General Assembly ... two from industrial countries and one each from Africa, Asia, and Latin America."[35]

MANAGING THE GLOBAL ECONOMY AND THE GLOBAL ECOLOGY

Even without any form of world government, all but the most ardent apostles of Adam Smith might agree that the late twentieth-century global economy has evolved to a point where it could profit from more effective mechanisms of higher management. And (perhaps especially without any world government) global economic management is probably the only effective approach to managing the global environment as well.

Even for those who are not ideologically or otherwise obsessed by the risks of distorting free markets, the right mechanisms are far from obvious. Even if they were more obvious than they are, the practical problems of creating them are, again, extremely difficult at best.

As a case in point, as noted by the Commission on Global Governance, the

> world's ten biggest economies on a purchasing power parity basis include China, India, Brazil, and Russia ... Yet none of these participate in the Group of Seven, all are under-represented in terms of votes in relation to their population and economic weight in the Bretton Woods institutions, and China and Russia are not yet members of GATT. It is a matter of common interest that the major players in the global economy be fully involved in decision-making on common problems.[36]

One problem here is that national governments are not the key players in even the attenuated free-market world economy that now does reach more or less around the globe. The business enterprises and financial institutions at the heart of the action do not focus on "purchasing power parity" – a statistic that (somewhat artificially) takes account of international differences in prices. They worry about what they have in or out of their pockets at the end of the day. And the standard-measure GNP data provided by the World Bank (and illustrated in Table 2, page 14) reflect the numbers that count in their real world.

When the Group of Seven replaced the United States as the *ad hoc* global economic manager in the 1970s, it was not because the U.S. government decided that this would be better as "a matter of common interest." It was because "it had no option but to share the stage and, indeed, to plead for the co-operation of Germany and Japan."[37] Even inside the G7 it is still the institutions of the United States, Japan, and Germany that call the main shots today (insofar as anyone does at all). Effective high managerial power in a market economy naturally gravitates towards those players who are big enough to move the market.

In fact, China – for one – does seem on the verge of acquiring economic power of this magnitude. Even in terms of standard-measure GNP numbers, it has recently replaced Canada as the world's seventh-largest national economy. During the spring of 1995 the former Canadian prime minister Brian Mulroney, in a speech in Beijing, suggested that "China should be asked to join all leading international organizations" and "should also be invited to the G7 summit as an observer, as Russia is."[38] While concerned that China "agrees to play by accepted international rules," even the U.S. business press knows that the new World Trade Organization "really can't afford to exclude China."[39] A few months after Mulroney's speech, Jeffrey Garten, U.S. undersecretary of commerce for international trade, "said that if he were writing a novel about a new G7 for the 21st century," the group would include the U.S., Germany, Japan, China, India, Brazil, and Renato Ruggerio, head of the WTO.[40]

The Group of Seven as it now exists has recently taken some interest in the increasingly controversial problems of the anarchic international financial system bequeathed by the unilateral U.S. abandonment of the Bretton Woods stabilization mechanism in 1971. One now long-standing approach to these problems is the U.S. economist James Tobin's proposal "to tax or charge for foreign currency transactions." The argument here is that a tax of this sort would "improve the efficiency" of the "largest global market" and act to stabilize "a good deal of speculative trading, which is too short-term to reflect fundamental economic factors." It "might also enable governments to pursue more independent monetary policies by allowing a greater disparity of short-term interest rates." Yet as the recent report of the Commission on Global Governance itself points out:

> Such a tax faces considerable practical problems ... not the least being the decentralized, unregulated, electronically mediated nature of foreign exchange markets in most industrial countries, with no paper trails to provide a tax base. There would also be an incentive to move markets to tax havens.[41]

A related issue involves the large debt loads that various third-world governments found themselves suddenly saddled with during the initial phases of the new symbiosis between transnational corporations and less-developed countries in the 1970s and early 1980s. Some have argued that since many of the specific debts involved are essentially artificial consequences of speculative volatility in the anarchic international financial system (some of which has even been stimulated by criminal activity), they should simply be cancelled[42] (or defaulted on – as the state of Mississippi defaulted on its debts to British banks in the nineteenth century). In the wake of the mid-1990s currency crisis in Mexico, the U.S. business press urged that the International Monetary Fund "should have been operating an early warning system that detects problems in emerging economies before they become catastrophes."[43]

The Group of Seven itself has recently begun to contemplate action on the most pressing issues of this sort. The most ardent global governance advocates are pointing to the need for some new high managerial institution in the global economy. Some call for a "new Bretton Woods" stabilization system.[44] The Commission on Global Governance has proposed a new "Economic Security Council ... established as a distinct body within the UN family, structured like the Security Council, though not with identical membership and independent of it." As a bow to ecological concerns, one of the "ESC's tasks" would be to "provide a long-term strategic policy framework in order to promote stable, balanced, and sustainable development." The process of establishing the Economic Security Council would include exploring "the creation of an international corporate tax base among multinational companies."[45]

THE LIMITATIONS OF "GLOBAL CIVIL SOCIETY"

Even so rigorously realistic an analyst as Henry Kissinger has noted that, as matters stand,

> the international economic system operates – if at all – as crisis management. The risk is, of course, that some day crisis management may be inadequate. The world will then face a disaster its lack of

foresight has made inevitable ... My major point is that the world needs new arrangements.⁴⁶

Such new arrangements, however, will not come about until those who have the power to move the markets of the global economy see it as in their interests to create them – and to abide by what they create. The original Bretton Woods management system was possible because the United States had a larger economy than the rest of the world combined at the end of the Second World War. Even without the reconstitution of the present Group of Seven, there are more major players today. And having more players means it is more difficult to achieve agreement on collective action.

For a time in the spring of 1995 the U.S., Japan, and Germany did nothing about speculative pressure on the U.S. dollar because they could see no collective action that was in their individual interests.⁴⁷ In trying to resolve its chronic trade deficit with Japan, it sometimes seems, Washington may even be prepared to withdraw from the fledgling World Trade Organization,* and thus "undermine a new world trading system it took seven years to negotiate."⁴⁸ The vast domestic market in the United States is still important to many international economic players. Selling into this market has been an alluring development strategy for rising and mature national economies in various parts of the third and first worlds. From Washington's own point of view, the special foreign attractions of the U.S. domestic market lend weight to the argument that bilateral talks between the U.S. government and troublesome U.S. trading partners "may reap benefits faster than the unwieldy WTO."⁴⁹

One key problem of global governance in the face of such inescapable real-world pressures is that it lacks what the language of the domestic American political system would call a credible political base. In response, as it were, international activists have argued that "among the important changes of the past half century has been the emergence of a vigorous global civil society, assisted by ... communications advances ... which have facilitated interaction around the world." In 1909 there were a mere 176 international non-governmental organizations. By 1993 the number had risen to 28,900. The recent vigour of the new global civil society "reached a high point in Rio with the UN Conference on Environment and Development in 1992," where "more than 1,400 NGOs were accredited to the official conference and thousands more participated in the parallel Global Forum."⁵⁰

---

* Or at least keep its distance. In the summer of 1995, for example, the United States remained aloof from a WTO trial accord, to begin opening up global trade in local financial services in 1996 and 1997.

Realistic citizens of the world nonetheless appreciate the continuing limitations of this kind of global civil society. Democracy, as global governance advocates often claim, means more than voting politicians into office. But it also means more than being accredited to attend global conferences by international bureaucrats with only the vaguest and most symbolic forms of accountability to anyone. It seems no exaggeration to suggest that the overwhelming majority of people even in the electronic global village of today have not heard of the Commission on Global Governance.

Many who participate in the non-governmental organizations of the global civil society are doing public-spirited work for the emerging global community. There have been encouraging examples of successful "unarmed forces"[51] in the planet's recent history. Resolute masses of ordinary people *can* generate real political power when enough of them unite behind a common cause.[52] The sad events of 4 June 1989 in Beijing showed how impotent popular power can be in the face of armed suppression by resolute authorities, but with only a surprisingly few exceptions the collapse of the totalitarian regimes in Eastern Europe during the same year took place without the firing of a single shot. For whatever good or bad reasons, the United Nations has been less of a failure than the League of Nations. The present UN organization does need major reform, but much useful discussion about just what this might involve is under way. The global village has so far avoided a monumentally destructive third world war. Spaceship earth has not yet quite succumbed to ecological catastrophe. It is important to keep working at global governance. The world today is lucky that so many people are doing just that.

It would be monumentally naive, however, to imagine that the global civil society on the eve of the new millennium is in anything more than a very early and insubstantial stage of a very long and arduous process of development. Ordinary citizens of the world cannot seriously rely on global governance to look after the problems of today's accelerated globalization process that affect their interests. We have only just begun to address the daunting challenge of creating an authentically global political order that is not also a forbidding nightmare of tyranny. The "world at large" is still in its infancy – still too new to know how to look after itself.

It will be a long time yet before we have a workable global political system that can even begin to manage the planet, in the real universal interests of (as the present UN Charter has it) "We the Peoples, of the United Nations." The plain truth is that global governance is still largely a branch of political science fiction.

Table 9
The Twenty Largest National Economies: GNP Per Capita, 1993
("Standard Measure" and "Purchasing Power Parity" Compared)

Standard Measure	$ (U.S.)	Pur. Power Parity*	$ (U.S.)
Switzerland	36,410	United States	24,750
Japan	31,450	Switzerland	23,620
Sweden	24,830	Japan	21,090
United States	24,750	Germany	20,980
Germany	23,560	Canada	20,410
France	22,360	France	19,440
Belgium	21,210	Australia	18,490
Netherlands	20,710	Belgium	18,490
Canada	20,670	Italy	18,070
Italy	19,620	Netherlands	18,050
United Kingdom	17,970	United Kingdom	17,750
Australia	17,510	Sweden	17,560
Spain	13,650	Spain	13,310
South Korea	7,670	South Korea	9,810
Argentina	7,290	Argentina	9,130
Mexico	3,750	Mexico	7,100
Brazil	3,020	Brazil	5,470
Russian Federation	2,350	Russian Federation	5,240
China	490	China	2,120
India	290	India	1,250

* "Purchasing power parity" is defined as the number of units of a country's currency required to buy the same amounts of goods and services in the domestic market as one dollar would buy in the United States.

Source: The World Bank Atlas 1995.

CHAPTER SEVEN

THE FATE OF THE NATIONAL STATE

ARE WE SERIOUS ABOUT DEMOCRACY?

"The markets are very inefficient and manic-depressive. And wrong a lot."

Charles H. Brandes, 1995[1]

If global governance is still far too fragile and underdeveloped – and likely to remain this way far into the foreseeable future – just where can the ordinary citizen of the world turn, as he or she tries to cope with the accelerated globalization process of today? Apostles of Adam Smith would simply say the free market. A few steps beyond this, Christopher Farrell puts his faith in "the liberal ideas of the bourgeoisie, from free trade to democracy." Others (having lost faith in the real world altogether) would counsel one or another form of religion. Someone who lives in Belgium or Luxembourg might recommend the European Union.

The most essential truth is probably V.S. Naipaul's point that the "world is too various." To start with, the right place to turn will depend on just where the citizen involved happens to live. My own sense is that over large parts of the globe today the right place will be a suitably updated version of the traditional nation-state (which is not in fact at all as traditional as we sometimes pretend). This may seem to fly in the face of much recent debate and discussion,[2] since some parts of what might be called the death-of-the-nation-state argument make sense. But my contention is that other parts of that argument are mixing up political forests and economic trees. From another standpoint again, it could be said that in some respects the *nation-state*, which implies some (often fictional) common ethnic descent among its members, is dying. In other respects, however, it is rapidly being replaced by a very close relative that might be called the national state, which simply refers to the government of a geographic space, somewhere in between the local community and the world at large.

THE HISTORIC PRIMACY OF POLITICS

As advocates of global governance do recognize, economic institutions are no more suited than political institutions to manage everything in human life. Even more crucially – and even when they are guided by Adam Smith's invisible hands – economic institutions do not create and sustain themselves.

Franz Neumann, a German labour lawyer who was proscribed by Hitler in the 1930s and finally chose to live in the United States, put this last point succinctly in the early 1950s. A competitive society especially, he explained, "requires general laws." Freedom "of the commodity market, freedom of the labor market, free entrance into the entrepreneurial class, freedom of contract, and rationality of the judicial responses in disputed issues" all require "the creation of a legal order which will secure the fulfilment of contractual obligations." For free markets to work efficiently (or profitably), the "expectation that contractual obligations will be performed must be made calculable."

Historically (first in Western Europe several hundred years ago and then ultimately all around the world), the work of establishing such a calculable legal order has been undertaken by the sovereign state. Through the "monopoly of coercion" that only it can legitimately command, the nation-state has "created large economic areas and integrated them legally and administratively" to secure the strategic political framework without which "our modern commercial and industrial society" would be impossible.[3]

As the global movement for free-market reform since the late 1970s makes clear, nothing in the accelerated globalization process of the late twentieth century has changed the strategic role of the national state in this respect. As the Shell Oil planners' Barricades scenario so ominously implies, what may or may not be the new order of global free trade remains precariously dependent on the willingness of the more than 100 sovereign national states who signed the final text of the GATT Uruguay Round to abide by their commitments.

As Franz Neumann's sad personal experience in Germany between the two world wars made so obvious to him, this ultimate "primacy of politics over economics" has always been "a fact, which was at times glossed over, at times openly recognized. In the structure of totalitarian states the circumstances are so clear that one need not waste many words. In the structure of democratic states the circumstances are frequently concealed through ignorance." However, "even in the period of unlimited Manchesterdom" (or in what some still see as the nineteenth-century golden age of economic freedom and limited government in the United Kingdom and the United States)* "politics had the hegemony."[4]

---

* In an earlier era the free-market ideological doctrines introduced by Adam Smith were often known as those of "the Manchester School," after the leading English city of nineteenth-century liberal capitalism and the first industrial revolution.

In pondering the depths of what this means, one can still be helped by some imagery from the "dying culture" of which T.S. Eliot's poetry is a "brilliant efflorescence." This culture *is* dying, and it is sexist and patriarchal and a number of other reprehensible things as well, but there is a side to it (in both its European and non-European variations) that remains deeply rooted in some persistent facts of human behaviour. And as yet no one has discovered a workable alternative to this side of all the world's dying cultures. Put simply, it is part of the cross mere humanity continues to bear ("the 'bondage' of earthly existence"[5] which can only be transcended in another realm) that raw physical force is the decisive last resort of human action. In the more technical language of the most frank and robust traditions of twentieth-century political science, the methods of political power, which "range from the marginal case of killing to the marginal case of education,"[6] tend to make all politics, as George Orwell once wearily observed, "of their nature ... inseparable from coercion and fraud."[7] Yet – ever since Eve gave Adam the apple, as the Judaeo-Christian regional tradition has it – power of this sort has remained the ultimate human power on the planet. And around the globe today, the sovereign national state remains the only institution that can legitimately use this power.

THE RECENT GLOBALIZING EROSION OF THE NATIONAL STATE

If all this is true, why has there been so much recent talk about the death of the nation-state? Put simply, the dramatically accelerated globalizing trends of the late twentieth century have presented the governments of nation-states virtually everywhere with some major new challenges and dilemmas. According to the Commission on Global Governance, although "states retain sovereignty," national "governments have suffered an erosion in their authority."[8]

In fact "authority" is not quite the right word. The forces at the bottom of the erosion are fundamentally economic. They owe a lot to the new transportation, communication, and information technologies of the third and fourth industrial revolutions. And they have at least three key operational dimensions: the growth of transnational corporations; the spread of "freer" international trade regimes; and the rise of anarchic forms of a new global economic sovereignty, in the international financial system.

To start with, "all economic activity takes place within national boundaries," and all business corporations begin as national corporations, created within and in some senses by the political framework of the nation-state.[9] Because they have in some degree created them, national governments can in some degree control "their own" national corporations.

The evolution of a national into a transnational corporation, however, diminishes the control of one nation-state by creating opportunities for placing strategic elements of the corporate structure under the control of another nation-state. Transnational corporation A, for example, can escape government regulations to protect labour interests in country X by shifting its production for country X consumer markets to country Y, where the national government is less concerned about labour standards.

This strategy will not work if the government of country X erects high tariff walls against exports of transnational corporation A's production in country Y. The spread of freer international trade regimes since the first GATT round in 1947, however, has diminished the control of national governments in this respect as well.

The GATT Uruguay Round agreement as well as recent regional agreements – which address both traditional tariff and so-called non-tariff barriers to international trade – have brought additional pressures on what the U.S. economic geographer Nancy Ettlinger has called "national modes of production." Even countries as similar as the United States, the United Kingdom, Germany, and Italy have traditionally had "fundamentally different production systems."[10] Different national governments, responding to different national cultures, have presided over the creation of these systems. To some as yet unclear degree, the new trade agreements of the 1990s are pushing national modes of production towards some new "harmonized" international mode (and/or a number of new harmonized regional modes), over which most national governments can exert far less influence.

To ice at least someone's cake, the new anarchic international financial system, created both by the U.S.A.'s unilateral withdrawal from its Bretton Woods commitments in 1971 and by the microelectronic miracles of the fourth industrial revolution, has itself increasingly acquired new degrees of control over national governments.

Since the earliest beginnings of both capitalism and the globalization process, national financial systems have had some considerable dependence on international networks, presided over by the strongest national (and imperial) economic powers of the day.[11] One novel feature of the globalized international financial system of the late twentieth century is that there are virtually no strongest national or imperial powers presiding over it. According to its most severe critics, the system is "dominated by speculators" and effectively managed by "the proverbial 25-year-old trader in red suspenders."[12] These traders and speculators, attuned to little more than the narrowest logic of reaping profits (or losses) from short-term money transactions, have powerful new high-technological tools at their fingertips. As the chief executive officer of the Bank of Montreal explained to a Canadian Senate committee studying Canada's bank-regulatory apparatus in 1985:

I can hide money in the twinkling of an eye from all of the bloodhounds that could be put on the case, and I would be so far ahead of them that there would never be a hope of unravelling the trail. I am not kidding you. Technology today means that that sort of thing can be done through electronic means.[13]

National governments increasingly depend on this anarchic monetary pinnacle of the global economy to finance their activity. And, as already noted in chapter 3, some argue that this increasing dependence is promoting the rise of "a new class of stateless legislators," who with "the power of the purse ... check governments' ability to tax, spend, borrow, or depreciate their debts through inflation."[14]

THE NATIONAL STATE AND WHAT EVERYONE REALLY WANTS

The worldwide erosion of national economic power points to key issues that successful nation-states of the future are going to have to wrestle into some neutral corner. There are nonetheless crucial senses in which economic power remains subject to the historic "primacy of politics over economics." Setting aside the constraints on the use of military might induced by the advent of nuclear weapons, there has been (alas, some would say) no fundamental erosion of the nation-state's monopoly of legitimate physical force.

Transnational corporations, new free-trade agreements, and new kinds of free-market international financial networks are creating a global economic system that constrains some historic options of national governments. But the lure of this system is tied nevertheless to essentially political arguments for a particular global economic development strategy – on which the jury is still out. The international money manager George Soros has recently argued that national leaders are now faced with a situation where "you can opt out of the system ... but, if you do, that destroys prosperity."[15] Yet the real extent and nature of this prosperity is not at all clear, and insofar as the system actually is working to increase global prosperity, it is equally unclear that it is working in the way some of its most enthusiastic supporters claim.

For the moment, much (or even most) of the third and old second worlds are "buying into" the system, because this now seems the most realistic hope for spreading the machine civilization around the globe. The crucial failure of third- and old second-world national governments since 1945 has been their inability to deliver the blessings of the machine civilization that everyone everywhere wants. One striking survey-research statistic from the NAFTA debate in North America was that "a majority of Mexicans would actually favor their country merging with the United States if, by doing so, their standard of living would increase significantly."[16]

It does seem increasingly indisputable that the new global economic system has started to deliver the benefits of the machine civilization to some parts of the so-called third world – especially in Asia and, to a lesser extent, in Latin America. And though the experience in the new national states that have arisen from the ashes of the Soviet Union has for the most part not been promising, it is far too early to rush to judgments here. Tropical Africa, however, is a large region of the world where the new system has not even begun to work, despite the efforts of various African national governments to create hospitable political regimes.

Moreover, both the first-world case of Japan and the third-world cases of the newly industrializing economies in Asia more generally raise doubts about the entire thesis of the globalizing economic erosion of the national state. (The thesis itself owes a great deal to Anglo-American globalization ideology in the United States and the United Kingdom, mediated by the quite unique experience of the rise of the European Union.) Even today, "when push comes to shove, the Japanese, perhaps more than most," still "look toward their government for protection and succor."[17] In such places as South Korea, Malaysia, Indonesia, and even China, there seems a sense in which the new globalizing trends of the late twentieth century are actually being used to build and strengthen new national states.[18]

A final point is obvious enough as well. Even on the most optimistic assumptions about the capacity of the new global economic system to spread the benefits of the machine civilization around the planet, how will newly developing third-world (or even second-world) national states cope with the historically demonstrated tendency of the industrial revolution "especially in its early stages, to widen the gap between rich and poor and sharpen the cleavage between employer and employed"?[19] This question draws attention to how this historical tendency has been handled in first-world national states that have already had their industrial revolutions. It also pushes any preliminary evaluation of the new global economic system in still more complicated and uncertain directions again.

CAPITALISM, SOCIAL POLICY, AND DEMOCRACY

The system that the third and second worlds are now buying into is not the old "high imperial" system of the 1870–1913 globalization era, which began to diffuse the then quite new machine civilization globally in a way that redounded to the particular advantage of first-world countries. Although there are still enormous inequities, the two major waves of decolonization after the Second World War, the OPEC adventures of the 1970s, and the new technologies of the third and fourth industrial revolutions have created the beginnings of a more geographically balanced modern world economy.

This points to the most rational source of the pressures brought to bear on first-world national governments by today's globalization process. If citizens of the third and old second worlds are ultimately to have the same access to the consumer goods of the machine civilization as citizens of the first world, the most crucial global economic objective is to produce enough to go around. Both the leaders and the led in first-world countries are now having to confront the prospect that George Orwell so presciently anticipated in the late 1940s (and that we have already noted in the second chapter of this book):

> Quite largely, indeed, the workers were won over to Socialism by being told that they were exploited, whereas the brute truth was that, in world terms, they were exploiters. Now, to all appearances, the point has been reached when the working-class living standard *cannot* be maintained, let alone raised. Even if we squeeze the rich out of existence, the mass of the people must either consume less or produce more.[20]

Put another way, even for socialists the overriding global economic problem of the late twentieth and twenty-first centuries is not how to redistribute the wealth that already exists, but how to create new wealth, without which (as Orwell also explained) "economic equality merely means common misery."[21] And this helps explain why many citizens of first-world national states in the 1980s and 1990s have found themselves facing eroding incomes and increasingly more work and less leisure (or even worse, more unemployment), despite ubiquitous prophecies in exactly the opposite direction during the 1960s and early 1970s.

At the same time, as Orwell himself would understand, world history has never been quite as simple as all this suggests.[22] There are many good reasons to suspect that some of today's first-world leaders are exaggerating the rational dimensions of global competition to advance a narrower ideological agenda. At its most aggressive the agenda urges that it is now altogether impossible to sustain the social policies virtually all first-world national governments have developed to combat the historical tendency of the industrial revolution to widen the gap between rich and poor.

Just where rationality ends and ideology begins in this particular debate is not easy to judge, but a few things do seem obvious. One is that continuing technological advance, according to its most widely accepted justification, is supposed to allow us to escape the finite limits of the planet's resources – to produce more in such a way as to increase living standards in the third world without at the same time decreasing those in the first world. Another is that spreading the machine civilization around the globe will hardly be progressive if it means that, in order for new *minorities* in the third world to get rich, old *majorities* in the first world will have to become poor again (and if this is true, why should *majorities* even in the third world have any more interest in this new global economic-development strategy than they had in the old high imperial one?).

A related concern raises problems even for Christopher Farrell's faith in "the liberal ideas of the bourgeoisie, from free trade to *democracy*." Although current advocates of global governance urge that democracy means more than electing politicians to office, the dominant assumption in first-world countries since the end of the Second World War has been that electing politicians to office is one of democracy's essential meanings. This is the only workable "political method" for ensuring that the national state's monopoly of legitimate force is made accountable to the majority of its citizens.[23]

In this same context, the first-world democratic capitalist social-welfare states that were consolidated during the generation that followed the Second World War reflected the rising power of increasingly more-educated democratic majorities. To contend in current public policy debate that postwar social-policy expenditure has more recently ballooned beyond the financial capacity of first-world national economies – and that electorates that insist on ignoring this will only impoverish themselves still more – is well within democratic traditions. (And, as recent political trends in many first-world national states make clear enough, this is an argument to which many democratic voters are sensitive.)

To say, however, that "globalization" means that elected politicians in today's first-world democracies – and the electorates who put them into office – no longer have the power to make fundamental social-policy decisions is to say that globalization means democracy is no longer possible as well. With problems of exactly this sort in mind, the Canadian Finance Minister J.L. Ilsley, in introducing legislation implementing the new International Monetary Fund in Canada's House of Commons in 1945, stressed that

> the Fund is specifically enjoined from concerning itself with domestic policies ... The fact that a country has adopted a social security programme ... can be no concern of the Fund's if that member should subsequently apply for a change in its exchange rate.[24]

THE NATIONAL STATE AND THE DEMOCRATIC POLITICAL SYSTEM

At this point in the argument it becomes absolutely impossible to keep up even the analytic pretense that we are all neutral citizens of the world. To get to the very bottom of the real problems of globalization at the edge of the new millennium, we must each think and speak in our own voices – with all the particular geographic and cultural baggage that the overwhelming majority of us continue to bear.

In this quite specific context, it seems to me, it is not easy to judge just how serious we in the so-called West really are about democracy today – on either the right or the left. The title of the Hungarian-American historian John Lukacs's modern history of the United States – *Outgrowing Democracy* – is suggestive in this respect.[25] I find it disturbing as well.

My own view is that democratic government is the West's most valuable and convincing legacy to the emerging global, regional, and national cultures that the turmoil of our times is spawning. And though "the West" is also a "dying culture," its greatest legacy has earned the right to live on, into the new era of great transformation.

I do not think, however, that we who are fortunate enough to live in functioning national democracies should be wasting much time telling others to copy our form of government. I do not agree, for instance, with the editorialist in my local newspaper that "the West" should be urging "China to accept democracy."[26] The best way for those of us who believe in democracy to propagate our values worldwide is to lead by example at home – to show by how we run our own national societies in the tough new times of the information age that democracy in fact is the best form of government for the overwhelming majority of people.

In any case, for anyone who still believes in democracy, the national state itself remains a key global value because the national state remains the only viable real-world framework for the democratic political system. The United Nations may become more democratic in some more diffuse senses over the next few generations – and I hope it does – but it would be absurd to argue that it can become a serious real-world framework for any functioning democratic political system over any future time period that can be sensibly thought about today.

Then there is Hannah Arendt's view of the deep moral dangers in world government. And there is the important corollary of this view that the democratic political system is also the most realistic hope for redeeming the national state's own ominous monopoly of legitimate force – by grounding it in a secular morality that most people in a diverse population can honourably accept.

GLOBAL POWER IN LARGE NATIONAL STATES

For better or for worse, a belief in the value of the democratic political system and the national state does not have definitive implications for particular policy decisions. And at the moment, in first-world politics there seem to be no simple answers to thorny questions about social policy and economic development.

Consider, for instance, a view of current national problems in the United States advanced by an official of the Deutsche Bank in Germany, during the final stages of the NAFTA negotiations in the spring of 1993:

> In an international competition perspective, the problem is not so much that the American labour force is not producing quality products; it just is not producing the products that people want in sufficient numbers. Those products are not being marketed properly. They are management failures, not the failures of people on the assembly line. And one of the additional failures of American leadership in business and in public life has been that they have been practising a low-wage strategy over the last two decades. Indeed, that is one of the perspectives with which they engaged in the NAFTA negotiations: to keep further pressure on American salaries.[27]

Now consider a view of current national problems in Germany advanced by a U.S. business writer stationed there, in the spring of 1995:

> The German Auto Makers Federation (VDA) estimates that U.S. and Japanese unit labor costs will average 55% and 56%, respectively, of their German competitors' costs this year. The contrast with Eastern Europe is even more striking ... Adding to Germany's runaway costs is the gold-plated welfare state. Social levies already double average wage costs, but there is still no serious attempt to overhaul the system ... The key problem is that government, labor, and business all cling to the outmoded social consensus that ensured labour peace and nurtured economic success after 1945. Trouble is, the old social pact depended heavily on two hidden pillars: Relatively protected national markets and widespread capital controls that shielded Germans from too many outside pressures.[28]

My own view here is that the real location of the line between rationality and ideology in this broad social-policy-and-economic-development debate will remain uncertain for some time yet. But I do think that one thing can be predicted with considerable confidence. If the democratic majority in either the United States or Germany were to decide that the particular form of the globalization process ascendant today does run directly against its interests (even when all rational calculations about economic necessity in "world terms" have been allowed for), the governments of these two large and influential countries could mobilize enough power to sabotage the form and start changing it into something else again.

The present-day democracy in the United States probably even has the capacity to experiment with its own updated version of the isolationist Tokugawa shogunate strategy, practised so impressively by Japan in the seventeenth, eighteenth, and earlier nineteenth centuries. While five of the ten largest transnational corporations in the world today are headquartered in the United States, it is also true that "exports account for less than 10% of U.S. output, and imports of merchandise goods represent another 13%." As the U.S. Federal Reserve vice-chairman Alan Blinder pointed out in the spring of 1995: "We are considerably more closed than the globalizers would have us believe – and therefore more able to control our own destiny."[29]

TOWARDS SOME VAGUE CONCLUSIONS

As I tried to stress at the start, I do not think that many decisive answers to the questions raised by late twentieth-century globalizing trends are possible right now. The beginning of wisdom is *not* to pretend that things are clearer than they are.

The case of Germany, for instance, raises questions about national states and such potentially novel political entities as the European Union. (Will the political authority of traditional nation-states increasingly be usurped by supra-national organizations or regional super-states like the EU? If this does happen, what will be the fate of the present national cultures in such places as Germany – or Italy or France?) My own tentative view is that, as a matter of consuming interest, the relevance of such questions is largely confined to Europe. And for the EU to have real weight as some new form of regional super-state, it would have to accept full members from Africa and the Middle East (along with the former totalitarian regimes in Eastern and Central Europe).*

---

* In fact, the current provisions of the Lomé Convention, which offer European trade and aid support for most of Africa and various small places in the Caribbean and the Pacific, are scheduled to expire in 2003. And in the 1990s view of some Europeans "the Lomé measures flout Gatt's free-trade principles" (see Marina Warner, "Diary," *London Review of Books* 25 May 1995, 25). Other Europeans are looking forward to the 1996 "intergovernmental conference on economic and monetary union, and on reform of the institutions of the European Union, in preparation for the next enlargement towards Central and Eastern Europe" (see John Godfrey, "Looking to 1996," *Times Literary Supplement,* 28 July 1995, 31). Still others

As matters stand, what Europe may or may not be heading towards politically looks a little more like a multilingual version of the United States, which (presumably everyone would agree) is a large national and not a regional state. A related and in some respects more apt analogy may be the present-day multilingual large national state of India, which, as Indians often explain in conversation, is really more like Europe than like Germany or France.

This raises the final question of just how national states are defined in our own time, and just what this definition means. The most obvious (and sensible) definition here is that a national state is a political organization that belongs to the United Nations. In this respect the UN over the past half-century has been a raging and unqualified success – and that is no small achievement. The national state in the global village of today is "a by-product of the world order itself, the system and general assumptions of the states congregated ... together in the United Nations Organisation."[30]

A mere glance at the current roster of UN members will reveal that the national state at the edge of the new millennium is a highly varied phenomenon. Singapore, a mere dot on the map with a population of less than 3 million people, is an important national state today. Another is China, which commands the world's third-largest geographic territory and its overwhelmingly largest population of almost 1.2 billion people. According to international legal fiction, all national states are equal. Of course, this cannot possibly be true in practice. Some national states are so small that they are forever destined to be fundamentally dependent on larger ones. Yet, like all legal fictions, the principle of the equality of sovereign national states has its uses.*

A quick tabulation of the dates of admission of present-day UN member states also makes clear that more than 70 percent have joined since the establishment of the organization in 1945. Twenty-eight current UN member states actually joined up as recently as the four-year period from 1990 to 1993. It is a simple fact as well that there has been some considerable shift-

---

(from page 115) anticipate that a November 1995 conference of the EU and twelve of its southern Mediterranean neighbours (including Egypt, Israel, Jordan, Morocco, Syria, and Tunisia) may or may not "usher in a new era of close economic, political and security co-operation across the Mediterranean" – that will see the EU "play a bigger role in the region ... as a counterbalance to the United States" (see Jeremy Lovell, "EU meeting seen as turning point," *Globe and Mail,* 21 August 1995, B9).

* The Principality of Liechtenstein, which became a UN member state in 1990, has a population of about 30,000 people. It has a customs and monetary union with Switzerland, which has administered its postal services since 1921 as well. One of the uses of national sovereignty here is that Liechtenstein also has low taxes and serves as a convenient headquarters for various transnational corporate organizations.

ing-about of national state names and boundaries during the past half-century. Two of close to a dozen examples in a recent UN handbook dramatize the point:

> The Federal Republic of Germany and the German Democratic Republic were admitted to membership in the United Nations on 18 September 1973. Through the accession of the German Democratic Republic to the Federal Republic of Germany, effective from 3 October 1990, the two German States have united to form one sovereign State.

> The Federation of Malaya joined the United Nations on 17 September 1957. On 16 September 1962, its name was changed to Malaysia, following the admission to the new federation of Singapore, Sabah (North Borneo) and Sarawak. Singapore became an independent State on 9 August 1965 and a United Nations Member on 21 September 1965.[31]

To have lived in a national state like Canada over the past few decades is to appreciate that there will likely be more shifting-about of this sort in the future – and that one might find oneself directly affected. Canada is not the only place where recent globalizing trends have somewhat ironically been perceived as incubators for new national states. Even in the United Kingdom, the "so-called 'European debate' is part of a tortured national self-examination, an English, Scottish, Welsh and Irish agonizing about self."[32] European integration in the 1990s has already been accompanied by the creation of four very small new European UN member states.

In this same context, as important as they may become in other ways, there is not really a great deal of evidence to suggest that such recent creations as AFTA, NAFTA, and MERCOSUR (or even the EU itself) are the authentic germs of overweening new regional super-states.* The Hanseatic League was an important north European trading organization during the earlier phases of the historic globalization process – how many remember it today?[33]

---

* If it is correct that the EU is actually evolving in the direction of a large national state, this does raise the somewhat awkward question of whether smaller national states can be part of a larger one. Canadians have also had reasons to ponder a version of this question lately. At least on a miniature scale, the relationship between Liechtenstein and Switzerland would seem to suggest that the answer is yes.

"CIVIC TRIBALISM" IN THE GLOBAL VILLAGE

Like everything else, the nation-state has already begun to be transformed by globalizing pressures. To take the nation-state seriously as "a by-product of the world order itself" is something quite new, like the great majority of today's UN member states themselves. In this as in other respects the traditional nation-state is rapidly evolving into a new kind of national state.

For a rather long time now it has been "fashionable to defame the concept" of national sovereignty and hold it "responsible for all the ills of our present age."[34] There have certainly been reasons for this. "Nationalism" – in Orwell's sense of "the habit of identifying oneself with a single nation or other unit, placing it beyond good and evil and recognizing no other duty than that of advancing its interests" – has wreaked great havoc and destruction in the twentieth century.[35]

Historically the ethnic or tribal patina of the traditional nation-state has helped breed a kind of nationalism of which the world has already had too much. Assorted forms of old nationalist cultural backlash against changes brought about by the globalization process are casting too many dark shadows across the great transformation in world history that is under way.

Yet, as Orwell took equal pains to stress in the 1940s, it is not just the nation-state that breeds "nationalism" in this sense. Religious, political, and economic ideologies can do the same thing. "Nationalism ... does not necessarily mean loyalty to a government or a country, still less to *one's own country*, and it is not even necessary that the units in which it deals should actually exist."[36] It was the nation-state that created the Third Reich and even the "socialism in one country" of the U.S.S.R., but it was also other nation-states that crushed racist imperialism in the Second World War.

If we return to the roster of United Nations member states for our real-world definition of the nation-state today, the ethnic patina is considerably less than ubiquitous. Even where it is important, it is often (if not always) spread thinly. Some present-day advocates of new national states stress a new kind of "civic nation" – a "country defined by its institutions and laws rather than by its ethnos or imagined kinship. The only nationalism it can lay claim to will have a civic character, and political history must take the place of common descent or language."[37] An examination of the present UN roster suggests that perhaps a clear majority of the existing national states of the late twentieth century have already embraced some new civic model of this sort – in practice if not quite yet in theory.

When a phrase like "across the nation" is used by the mass media in the United States, it does in fact have more broad political than narrow ethnic connotations. A "national issue" in the U.S. does not mean an ethnic issue, but an issue that has enough breadth to interest the democratic political community at large. It is already not really possible to be ethnically American, or Brazilian, or Canadian, or Indian, or Micronesian, and on and on.

Now that we who live in North American countries have begun to explore the full range of our unifying political histories, we are starting to appreciate that some of our first tribes had their own civic dimensions. Historic North American Indian nations were not always strictly defined by ethnic or family identities. In times of war or social turmoil members of one tribe were sometimes adopted by another tribe. In one way or another, nations with depleted populations occasionally recruited new members from other nations. Several nations might form a defensive alliance or confederation. The growth of this kind of "civic tribalism" was sometimes accelerated by the arrival of the first Europeans (though not, it is worth stressing, by the Europeans themselves).[38]

In the midst of the inevitable ennui of the machine civilization, recapturing *some* parts of the tribal humanity of the "primitive" past could do almost everyone everywhere a great deal of good. The national political community in this sense is the human face of high technology.

THE NEXT SWING OF THE PENDULUM

There are of course more rather vague things that could be said. But this short book is almost at its end. The most decisive point is that historically the national state is itself a creation of the globalization process. It is the globalization process that has divided the planet into a formally uniform system of national states. In the spirit of Adam Smith's invisible hand, it is reasonable enough to guess that the history of globalization in this respect is trying to tell us something about how to deal with the problems it creates. As the globalization process continues to grow and develop, so will the national state.

I suspect this is the deepest significance of the debate about globalization and national governments that we are now in the middle of, in several different parts of the world. During the generation that followed the end of the Second World War we began to place too much faith in these governments. During the generation immediately after this (the one that started in the middle of the 1970s), we have begun to place too little. I am still wildly optimistic enough to believe that these swings of the pendulum have some point and serve some purpose. I think it will be a while yet before democratic government in my own country has taken all the steps it must to start growing stronger, in the interests of the great majority of the ordinary citizens it serves. But it should not be at all surprising if, at some point fairly early on in the new millennium, the pendulum starts to swing again.

Table 10
New Member States of the United Nations, 1990–1993

Member State	Date of Admission	1993 Pop. (000s)
AFRICA		
Eritrea	1993	3,200
Namibia	1990	1,565
ASIA		
South Korea	1991	44,056
North Korea	1991	23,051
Micronesia	1991	110
Marshall Islands	1991	53
EUROPE		
Czech Republic	1993	10,323
Slovakia	1993	5,345
Croatia	1992	4,788
Bosnia and Hercegovina	1992	4,383
Macedonia	1993	2,191
Slovenia	1992	1,993
Andorra	1993	63
Monaco	1993	31
Liechtenstein	1990	30
San Marino	1992	24
FORMER SOVIET UNION		
Uzbekistan	1992	21,969
Kazakhstan	1992	17,169
Azerbaijan	1992	7,435
Tajikstan	1992	5,684
Georgia	1992	5,456
Kyrgyz Republic	1992	4,512
Moldova	1992	4,356
Turkmenistan	1992	3,949
Lithuania	1991	3,747
Armenia	1992	3,731
Latvia	1991	2,588
Estonia	1991	1,546

Sources: United Nations; World Bank.

EPILOGUE

SOME PARTING THOUGHTS

"Your first impression is always wrong."
                                    Henry Kissinger, 1984[1]

If I have done my job well enough, readers are now beginning to make up their own minds about just what globalization is and whether it will work. I have only a little more to say myself — by way of summarizing what seems to me the essential thrust of the mild analytic argument in this book. I think there are two broad points worth special attention. The first comes in three parts; the second in a single lump.

Globalization, in the first place, is a confusing and contentious concept. To no small extent this is because, in the English-speaking world today, the word is used in too many different senses. Distinguishing among as few as three of them can at least avoid the most futile disputes.

My second point is simply that globalization as a historical process has been and will continue to be a fundamentally long-term phenomenon. Perhaps especially in North America, I think we could deal more effectively with globalization-related policy issues if, in our democratic public debate, we were somehow able to take better account of their longer-term context.

THE THREE SENSES OF GLOBALIZATION

Globalization as a Historical Process

One argument heard often enough lately is that globalization is essentially nonsense, or just plain wrong. While I think there are some respects in which this argument can be credible (and even rather apt), there is also a crucial sense in which it just cannot stand up. The dramatically accelerated globalization process of the late twentieth century is a real historical phenomenon and we are still in the middle of it. It is a strategic episode in an older story that stretches all the way back to the fifteenth century. And, allowing for the tiresome hyperbole of all such claims, I think Christopher Farrell is right when he suggests that the process has lately accelerated to the point where we now stand at the edge of a "great transformation in world history."

What globalization is in this sense is not all that hard to grasp. In one way or another, it has been in the air for a number of generations already (though not under quite so barbarous a name). When Bartholomew Diaz doubled the Cape of Good Hope in 1487 – or Columbus's three ships set sail in 1492 – no one in the world knew anything like the full extent of the planet's geography. Even in my parents' generation after the First World War there were still regions in the most northern part of North America that remained essentially un-mapped. At some point after the Second World War, however, the particular great adventure that Diaz began in 1487 came to an end. The planet earth now knew everything about itself, and by the 1960s it had begun to send human beings to the moon.

On the planet today, a few overarching aspects of real life actually have begun to unfold on something that approaches a global scale. As both Karl Marx and his late twentieth-century, free-market capitalist disciples would agree, "economics" tends to create the base for everything else, and it is the global economy that drives the commanding heights of the globalization process. Because the process is fundamentally historical, there has already been a dress rehearsal for the current high drama – in the earlier 1870–1913 era of accelerated globalizing trends. One key difference between then and now is that the 1870–1913 era was still dominated by the old sea-borne empires of Europe. As the historian John Bowle explained in the middle of the 1970s, "the overwhelming fact of our time is the rise of a global civilization." And, whatever else, "this global civilization will be a blend of cultures which will no longer be dominated by Europeans."[2]

To deny that all this has happened, that it is happening still – and that it has deep implications for everyone among us – is only to evade the facts of real life in the world today. It is also to cut oneself off from an enormously fascinating and engagingly mysterious new human adventure. And, again, I am still wildly optimistic enough to believe that this adventure holds out almost as many prospects for new kinds of hope and progress as it does for cynical and despairing doom and gloom.

Globalization as a Business Strategy

The bald-headed man at the back of the bus is not qualified to say much about the narrower meaning of globalization as a business strategy. I suppose the key question is: in the new era of great transformation before us, will those business enterprises that aspire to operate globally prove more successful, as businesses, than those that aspire to operate regionally, or nationally, or even locally? Or is some form of global expansion the best solution for first-world companies that have lately found themselves in new kinds of trouble?

No doubt the answers to this question have quite a lot to do with the real prospects for continuing global economic integration. According to

United Nations analysts: "Overall, as much as one-third of world output may now be under the direct governance" of transnational corporations, "with the indirect influence being almost certainly much greater."[3] Given the UN definition of a transnational corporation as a firm that simply operates in more than one country, it is difficult to know the extent to which this already quick-and-dirty statistic reflects genuinely global as opposed to merely regional reach. And I take Cyrus Freidheim seriously enough when he says that the "great idea" of the "global corporation" is still "largely a fiction" in the world today.

Inside my own country the Montreal-based management guru Henry Mintzberg has also recently said that the

> word "globalization" is pretentious. The globe usually starts around Seattle, goes to Vienna and then skips over to Tokyo, and is about 1,000 to 2,000 miles wide. I mean this is not the whole world ... There is only one global organization in that world – Greenpeace ... Coca-Cola is rather global, but a lot of other global organizations restrict themselves to developed countries.[4]

I do think Canada would be better off if more of its business enterprises were working harder to establish new relationships in developing countries. But the obvious rhetorical point here is that those who feel strongly about this should start their own businesses and do just that. I invest in emerging-market mutual funds and, alas, this is as close as I am ever likely to get.

My final somewhat gratuitous thought on this branch of the subject is that the fate of the new "Ford 2000" global-car strategy bears watching. Provisionally, I guess I would count myself among the sceptics, but my only real qualification for saying anything on this issue is that I once spent a summer working as an engine-dropper at a Ford plant in the Canadian city of Windsor (sometimes also known as "South Detroit"). I do think it is intriguing that Ford has recently set out on this bold new global path – led by Alex Trotman, who was born and grew up in the United Kingdom and then moved to the United States.

Globalization as an Ideology (Again)

Probably what most people who argue that globalization is essentially nonsense are talking about is a kind of ideological rhetoric that surfaced (especially in English-speaking countries, it seems to me) over the last few decades and has even gained considerable momentum in the more recent past. This sense of the word is obviously related to the other two, but it is quite distinct as well. You can accept globalization as a historical process (or perhaps even as a business strategy) without embracing any kind of globalization ideology.

Of course, an entire book could be written on various ideologies of globalization, and my final thoughts here are not at all comprehensive. The particular globalization ideology that interests me has two main distinguishing features. The first is a robust commitment to Adam Smith's vision of "economic freedom and limited government" as the best possible recipe for the future of the global economy. The second is a more than merely theoretical commitment to John Bowle's kind of rising "global civilization ... no longer ... dominated by Europeans" as the essential political and cultural framework for the new free-market global economy.

The first commitment has its roots in the experience of the 1970s and early 1980s; the second owes more to the later 1980s and early 1990s. Today the two commitments are linked by some notion akin to Christopher Farrell's rising multicultural "global middle class." And the present package rather quietly assumes that the key political questions for the future do turn around some (albeit highly limited – or perhaps even quite partial) form of global governance.

I have two observations about globalization ideology in this sense. The first is that it is largely an Anglo-American enterprise, particularly addressed to the problems created by the new economic forces of the 1970s, 1980s, and earlier 1990s for some strategic elites in the United States and the United Kingdom. The guiding pragmatic vision amounts to a post-colonial revival of the old British empire, with the former American colonies promoted to leader of the pack. The former subject peoples elsewhere have been raised to working partners. The former imperial metropolis takes on the part of the seasoned adviser, who still has wisdom to contribute but is too old to carry the ball. Alex Trotman's new Ford 2000 strategy fits the model nicely. So does the current fresh interest in "India, which will be not only the world's most populous country in another decade, but also one of the most technically advanced," and "is already designing computer chips for U.S. industry."[5] The spring 1995 week-long broadcast of David Letterman's New York–based television show from London adds a provocative cultural footnote.

This observation is not meant to cast moral aspersions on globalization ideology by linking it directly with the imperialism that Edward Said has called "an idea today so controversial, so fraught with all sorts of questions, doubts, polemics, and ideological premises as nearly to resist use altogether."[6] As someone who grew up in a former hinterland city of the British empire, I can sense some of the vision's visceral appeal. I think it does reflect a serious enough effort to transform imperialism into something more worthy of the imminent era of great transformation. Farrell and others like him are genuine about at least *their* version of "the right's" newly found multiculturalism. It may even be more apt to talk about "English-speaking" rather than "Anglo-American" globalization ideology.

The essential thrust of my second observation is nonetheless that this whole project is seminally naive. To start with, like so much else about "globalization" as the word is used today, it is not really *global* either – not rooted (as I also pointed out with regard to the parallel phenomena discussed in chapter 5) in some authentic concept of an altogether universal diverse global culture. At most English-speaking globalization ideology looks forward to a hybrid of global and regional cultures, with (say) the old geography of "the last and greatest of the European sea-borne Empires"[7] as the ultimate limit of its reach.*

Even within this limit, the late twentieth-century government of Malaysia that seeks membership in a new regional "caucus without caucasians" shows how many of the former subject peoples are not interested even in a multiculturally transformed revival of the old high imperial globalization process. George Orwell himself at "one time ... believed it might be possible to form the British Empire into a federation of Socialist republics." But "if that chance ever existed, we lost it ... by our attitude towards the coloured peoples."[8] The globalization process already has a long and often deeply bitter history behind it. The bitterness of its past constrains even the multicultural global future. The people who really want some future of this sort are migrating to the first world. The most plausible assumption is that the great majority who are not migrating want something else.

Finally, to return briefly to a point I argued at the end of chapter 7, I think that globalization ideology quite naively misreads the real longer-term direction in which the globalization process is pushing world politics. Shell Oil's Barricades scenario is too hyperbolic to serve as any realistic guide to the pragmatic future. My own sense is that at least a mild approximation of the ideals of "global free trade" is too much in the interests of too many powerful first-world institutions – and too many quite ordinary people everywhere – to be abandoned at the edge of the precipice. But I think Barricades does contain a few pregnant grains of truth. Today's accelerated globalization

---

* Taking a cue from Edward Said's reference to the present cultural diversity "even of France, which now contains large groups of immigrants," a Canadian is bound to note that the geographic reach could be extended somewhat by bringing La Francophonie into a "bilingual and multicultural" global strategy. This could probably be fairly described as "Western" rather than mere "English-speaking" globalization ideology. As a Canadian is also bound to note, it brings a fresh batch of practical and ideological problems. A "multilingual and multicultural" strategy, it seems safe to assume, would bring still more problems again.

process is also raising a few increasingly monumental problems for too many quite ordinary people – in all of the first, second, and third worlds. Not all that far down the road, we are probably going to find that in a great many cases the national state is still the most important political framework for dealing with these problems.

As Franz Neumann urged in the early 1950s, the international legal doctrine that sovereignty rests fundamentally with the national state is "basically anti-imperialist." And its "equalizing and limiting functions ... appear most strikingly when contrasted with the National Socialists' racial imperialism ... and with the doctrine of the sovereignty of the international proletariat."9 I suspect we are going to find that these equalizing and limiting functions will appear just as strikingly – and seem even more valuable – when they are contrasted with some new doctrine of the sovereignty of an international bourgeoisie.

Most simply, it is not at all clear that the democratic political system in the United States is either seriously capable of or genuinely interested in taking on the part that late twentieth-century English-speaking (or even "Western") globalization ideology assigns it. An America that takes its democratic traditions to heart, at least, will never be comfortable leading even a post-colonial and multicultural global empire. (And what other real traditions does America have?)*

THE LONG ROAD BEFORE US

My second broad summary point takes up at least a little less space. To start with, the long globalization process that began when Bartholomew Diaz doubled the Cape of Good Hope has now reached a juncture where the world at large is at the edge of a great transformation in its history. One thing this means is that in some important senses *all* the old cultures everywhere are dying.

At the same time, new global, regional, national, and local cultures are arising as well. And, along with the more obvious perplexing questions about economic development, social policy, and the environment, this is raising many new and difficult issues for public debate – perhaps especially in my own new regional universe in North America.

Decisions about these essentially cultural issues, or cultural and political issues, are more important than they sometimes seem, because they tend to define the frameworks within which such more immediately urgent matters

---

* The title of de Tocqueville's classic, after all, is *Democracy in America*, not *Capitalism in America* or *The Free-Market Society in America*.

as economic life unfold. I think we might handle decisions of this sort more effectively if we could cultivate more sensitivity about the longer-term puzzle of which they are mere pieces. Put as plainly as I can manage, the dramatically accelerated globalizing trends of the late twentieth century have rather suddenly opened a very long new road before us. Just where this road is leading is at the moment a great mystery. Much of this mystery is not even going to start to be dispelled, it seems to me, until we have travelled along the road a little further. And our impulse to rush to judgments may be the greatest danger we face today.

Perhaps the most naive aspect of globalization ideology, for instance, is that it is trying to strategize about a world that does not yet exist. I think it is true that "you cannot have globalization of economics without globalization of culture." But just what could some authentic global culture possibly be? To take just the most obvious point, how would it deal with the at once simple but highly complex fact that in the world at large today we do not all speak anything like the same language? In the face of such monumental questions, "right-wing" globalization ideology as a practical matter can only fall back on something that bears a close resemblance to the old imperialism that really did exist, but that the world at large now rightly regards as too repugnant for the future.

There are parallel forms of "left-wing" ideological thinking in the late twentieth-century air that can also only fall back practically on parallel repugnant old imperialisms. A fitting case in point at the end of this lean volume is the American feminist Daphne Patai's mid-1980s attack on George Orwell's life and work – *The Orwell Mystique: A Study in Male Ideology*. Patai virulently castigates Orwell's writing as fundamentally sexist, racist, anti-Semitic, homophobic, and militaristic. In fact, Orwell's adult personality was formed in the era between the two world wars, and he inevitably did share a few of the common prejudices of his day. But he also spent his earliest years in what amounted to a proto-feminist household. Very few male (and perhaps even female) writers of his time and place were less sexist, racist, and so forth – and more open to and presciently supportive of the new cultural values Patai herself claims to espouse – than George Orwell. Her attack only makes any kind of practical sense on the Stalinist political assumptions that have now been eclipsed (or at least ought to have been) by the end of the Cold War.[10]

What there is in Orwell's writing that Patai does logically find disturbing is a still highly relevant cultural critique of these same Stalinist assumptions (which, ironically enough, have one or two things in common with some assumptions of twentieth-century corporate capitalism). Writing in the mid-1980s, she was still trying to use these assumptions to implement her new values. If the collapse of the Soviet Union proves anything, however, it is that cultures are not just toys that we play with when we come home from work. We are nowhere near clever enough just to throw our dying cultures out and start afresh. We have to adapt them to new circumstances. Because our new circumstances are now so mysterious, we are moving into an era that will reward those who have prudence and patience and an appreciation for the value of time. "Backlash" is what happens when the great transformation moves too mindlessly and too fast.

Since the end of the Second World War we have faced the "danger that knowledge of the past may be neglected to the point that it ceases to serve the present and the future."[11] At our present juncture, I think, this danger has become acute. As matters stand in North America, we increasingly live in "a world where over-confident bigotry on the left faces over-confident bigotry on the right,"[12] and it is getting us nowhere. The overconfident ideological poses only reflect our deep lack of practical confidence about where we are going. We would have more confidence if we spent more time looking at where we have *really* been – and less time pondering abstract ideologies. In the end these ideologies no longer work at all, because our real future has become altogether too complicated for the now historically juvenile oversimplifications of either Karl Marx or Adam Smith.

What we probably do need are some new, historically rooted political ideas – as opposed to ideologies. Meanwhile, I think the *Taipan* authors, whose complimentary investment newsletter I received in the mail a while ago, have at least half a point. According to the global legends of our own time, the Chinese political leader Zhou Enlai was once asked what he thought of the French Revolution. He reflected for a moment and then said, "It is too early to tell." In this as in other respects, the West no doubt will find that it has a few things to learn from the wisdom of the East as we all move into the new era of world history that lies so mysteriously (and so intriguingly) ahead.

NOTES

Preface and Acknowledgments
1. *Men in Dark Times* (New York: Harcourt, Brace & World, 1968), 81.
2. As the local mayor and resident malaproprist of the 1950s, Allan Lamport, once explained: "Toronto is the city of the future – and always will be." On another occasion Mayor Lamport shrewdly observed that "no one should ever visit Toronto for the first time." What he was trying to say, of course, was that it takes a while to appreciate the virtues of the place. See John Robert Colombo, ed., *Colombo's Concise Canadian Quotations* (Edmonton: Hurtig Publishers, 1976), 213.

Prologue
1. V.S. Naipaul, *Finding the Center* (New York: Alfred A. Knopf, 1984), 79.
2. Christopher Farrell, "The Triple Revolution," *Business Week/21st Century Capitalism*, 18 November 1994, 16.
3. Debra Fleenor, "The Coming and Going of the Global Corporation," *Columbia Journal of World Business* 28, no. 4 (Winter 1993): 7.
4. Farrell, "The Triple Revolution," 16.
5. *Taipan*, Special 1995 Forecast Issue, 2. More serious readers of the Christian Bible would likely remember that the last book is known as "Revelation," not "Revelations."
6. With apologies, I have in fact rewritten the phrase slightly: Bagehot actually says "at the back of the omnibus" – a confusing term to late twentieth-century North American ears. See Walter Bagehot, *The English Constitution* (London: Collins, 1867, 1915, 1963), 247. As best I can judge, however, to revise further and say "bald-headed person" would offend those persons who are not men even more than leaving the anachronistically sexist "man" intact. The phrase refers, Bagehot goes on to explain, to "the ordinary mass of educated, but still commonplace mankind."
7. Quoted in Fleenor, "The Coming and Going of the Global Corporation," 9, 16.
8. Ibid., 15–16.
9. Farrell, "The Triple Revolution," 19, 22, 25.
10. Ibid., 25.
11. Joseph A. Schumpeter, *History of Economic Analysis* (New York: Oxford University Press, 1954), 1159.
12. United Nations Conference on Trade and Development, *World Investment Report 1994: Transnational Corporations, Employment and the Workplace* (New York and Geneva: United Nations, July 1994), 119.
13. Quoted in Fleenor, "The Coming and Going of the Global Corporation," 10.
14. Alfred G. Meyer, "The *Aufhebung* of Marxism," *Social Research* 43, no. 2 (Summer 1976): 201.
15. Robert Reich, *The Work of Nations* (New York: Alfred A. Knopf, 1991), 3, 8: cited in this case in Peter Dicken, "Global-Local Tensions: Firms and States in the Global Space-Economy," *Economic Geography* 70, no. 2 (April 1994): 102.
16. Sonia Orwell and Ian Angus, eds., *The Collected Essays, Journalism and Letters of George Orwell* (New York: Harcourt Brace Jovanovich, 1968), 3:305, 356–57. To cite Orwell in this context does not imply that he would have warmed to the late twentieth-century gospel of political correctness, especially in its more inane expressions.
17. Farrell, "The Triple Revolution," 25.
18. Richard O'Brien, *Global Financial Integration: The End of Geography* (New York: Council on Foreign Relations Press, 1992).
19. United Nations Conference on Trade and Development, *World Investment Report 1994*, 146.
20. J.M. Stopford and S. Strange, *Rival States, Rival Firms: Competition for World Market Shares* (Cambridge: Cambridge University Press, 1991), 233.
21. M.E. Porter, *The Competitive Advantage of Nations* (London: Macmillan, 1990), 19.
22. Canada is the home country for three of the world's one hundred largest transnational corporations (Seagram, Thomson Corporation, and Alcan Aluminum), according to the list in United Nations Conference on Trade and Development, *World Investment Report 1994*, 6–7. This list does not include financial corporations. A somewhat different kind of list is reported in Someshwar Rao, Marc Legault, and Ashfaq Ahmad, "Canadian-Based Multinationals: An Analysis of Activities and Performance," in Steven Globerman, ed., *Canadian-Based Multinationals* (Calgary: University of Cal-

gary Press, 1994), 84. According to this list, the ten largest "outward-oriented Canadian-based firms" are the Bank of Nova Scotia, Trilon Financial, Royal Trustco, Seagram, BCE, Thomson Corporation, Alcan Aluminum, Northern Telecom, Carena Developments, and Canadian Pacific.
23. Farrell, "The Triple Revolution," 24.
24. I have borrowed the phrase in quotation marks from John Bowle, *The Imperial Achievement: The Rise and Transformation of the British Empire* (Harmondsworth: Penguin Books, 1974, 1977), 554.
25. See, for example, Orwell and Angus, *The Collected Essays, Journalism and Letters of George Orwell*, 1:235.

Chapter 1: Imperial Echoes

1. Quoted in V.G. Kiernan, *European Empires from Conquest to Collapse, 1815–1960* (London: Fontana, 1982), 11.
2. Geoffrey Barraclough, ed., *The Times Atlas of World History* (London: Times Books, 1978), 13, 32, 38, 52. This is also the source for "our most immediate human ancestors some 40,000 years ago" (33).
3. J.H. Plumb, in his introduction to C.R. Boxer, *The Portuguese Seaborne Empire, 1415–1825* (London: Hutchinson, 1969), xxi.
4. See, for example, Mark A. Hartmann and Dara Khambata, "Emerging Stock Markets: Investment Strategies of the Future," *Columbia Journal of World Business* 28, no. 2 (Summer 1993): 86.
5. Immanuel Wallerstein, *The Modern World-System* (New York: Academic Press, 1974), 1:46–52. The discussion on China appears on pages 52–63.
6. Boxer, *The Portuguese Seaborne Empire*, 51.
7. J.H. Plumb in ibid., xxv.
8. John Bowle, *The Imperial Achievement: The Rise and Transformation of the British Empire* (Harmondsworth: Penguin Books, 1974, 1977), 107.
9. Wallerstein, *The Modern World-System*, 1: 51.
10. Samuel Eliot Morison, *The Oxford History of the American People* (New York: Oxford University Press, 1965), 164.
11. Bowle, *The Imperial Achievement*, 554.
12. Basil Williams [revised by C.H. Stuart], *The Whig Supremacy, 1714–1760* (Oxford: Oxford University Press, 1939, 1962, 1974), 363.
13. Immanuel Wallerstein, *The Modern World System* (San Diego: Academic Press, 1989), 3:129.
14. Barraclough, *Times Atlas of World History*, 232.
15. Plumb in Boxer, *The Portuguese Seaborne Empire*, xxv.
16. Bowle, *The Imperial Achievement*, 233.
17. Sonia Orwell and Ian Angus, eds., *The Collected Essays, Journalism and Letters of George Orwell* (New York: Harcourt Brace Jovanovich, 1968), 4:174.
18. Barraclough, *Times Atlas of World History*, 162.
19. Ron Chernow, *The House of Morgan: An American Banking Dynasty and the Rise of Modern Finance* (New York: Simon & Schuster, 1990), 5.
20. John Lukacs, *Outgrowing Democracy: A History of the United States in the Twentieth Century* (New York: Doubleday & Company, 1984), 97.
21. Harold Innis, *Essays in Canadian Economic History* (Toronto: University of Toronto Press, 1956, 1962), 407.
22. Edward Seidensticker, *Low City, High City – Tokyo from Edo to the Earthquake: How the Shogun's Ancient Capital Became a Great Modern City, 1867–1923* (New York: Alfred A. Knopf, 1983), vii.
23. Barraclough, *Times Atlas of World History*, 175.
24. United Nations Conference on Trade and Development, *World Investment Report 1994: Transnational Corporations, Employment and the Workplace* (New York and Geneva: United Nations, July 1994), 120.
25. Christopher Farrell, "The Triple Revolution" in *Business Week/21st Century Capitalism*, 18 November 1994, 22–23.
26. United Nations Conference on Trade and Development, *World Investment Report 1994*, 121.
27. Ibid., 122.
28. Barraclough, *Times Atlas of World History*, 240–41.
29. Ibid., 248.
30. Bernard Crick, *George Orwell: A Life* (Boston: Little, Brown and Company, 1980), 80–81.
31. Edward W. Said, *Culture and Imperialism* (New York: Vintage Books, 1993, 1994), 9, 5.
32. United Nations Conference on Trade and Development, *World Investment Report 1994*, 4–7.
33. Said, *Culture and Imperialism*, 5–6.
34. Ibid., xxi.

Chapter 2: Technology and the Machine Civilization

1. Sonia Orwell and Ian Angus, eds., *The Collected Essays, Journalism and Letters of George Orwell* (New York: Harcourt Brace Jovanovich, 1968), 1:235.
2. E.J. Hobsbawm, *Industry and Empire* (Harmondsworth: Penguin Books, 1968, 1969), 34. The exact dating of the industrial revolution can be somewhat controversial. For some more detailed discussion – with particular reference to the treatment of the phenomenon in Adam Smith's work – see Samuel Hollander, *The Economics of Adam Smith* (Toronto: University of Toronto Press, 1973, 1976), 21–22, 111–13, 236–41.
3. Hobsbawm, *Industry and Empire*, 54.
4. Orwell and Angus, *The Collected Essays, Journalism and Letters of George Orwell*, 1:397.
5. Ibid., 4:411.
6. Ibid., 1:445, 441.
7. J. Bronowski, *The Ascent of Man* (Boston: Little, Brown and Company, 1973), 165, 169, 165, 166.
8. Ibid., 162, 166.
9. Harold Innis, *The Bias of Communication* (Toronto: University of Toronto Press, 1951, 1971), 72.
10. Bronowski, *Ascent of Man*, 168.
11. Ibid.
12. A.L. Basham, *The Wonder That Was India* (New York: Taplinger Publishing Company, 1954, 1968), 498.
13. David C. Mowery and Nathan Rosenberg, *Technology and the Pursuit of Economic Growth* (Cambridge: Cambridge University Press, 1989), 21.
14. Hobsbawm, *Industry and Empire*, 59.
15. David S. Landes, *The Unbound Prometheus: Technological Change and Industrial Development in Western Europe from 1750 to the Present* (Cambridge: Cambridge University Press, 1969), 1, 4.
16. Ibid., 4.
17. Mowery and Rosenberg, *Technology and the Pursuit of Economic Growth*, 22.
18. Landes, *The Unbound Prometheus*, 7.
19. Paul Mantoux, *The Industrial Revolution in the Eighteenth Century* (London: Jonathan Cape, 1928, 1961), 27.
20. Joseph Schumpeter, *History of Economic Analysis* (New York: Oxford University Press, 1954), 391.
21. Mantoux, *The Industrial Revolution*, 35.
22. Abraham Rotstein, ed., *Beyond Industrial Growth* (Toronto: University of Toronto Press, 1976), ix.
23. Orwell and Angus, *The Collected Essays, Journalism and Letters of George Orwell*, 4:445, 81, 411, 427–28.
24. Ibid., 4:445
25. Landes, *The Unbound Prometheus*, 1.
26. United Nations Conference on Trade and Development, *World Investment Report 1994: Transnational Corporations, Employment and the Workplace* (New York and Geneva: United Nations, July 1994), 125. The quotation within the quotation is from Christopher Freeman, *Technology Policy and Economic Performance: Lessons from Japan* (London: Pinter, 1987), 130.
27. United Nations Conference on Trade and Development, *World Investment Report 1994*, 125.
28. Ibid., 125–26.
29. Hobsbawm, *Industry and Empire*, 59, 61.
30. Based on the 1992 ranking by foreign assets in United Nations Conference on Trade and Development, *World Investment Report 1994*, 6.
31. Raymond Vernon, *Storm over the Multinationals: The Real Issues* (Cambridge, Mass.: Harvard University Press, 1977), 19.
32. Organization for Economic Co-operation and Development, *Technology and the Economy: The Key Relationships* (Paris: OECD, 1992), 221.
33. Michael Ghertman and Margaret Allen, *An Introduction to the Multinationals* (London: Macmillan, 1982, 1984), 7.
34. Ibid., 9–10.

Chapter 3: Twists and Turns

1. "Towards a liberal Utopia: An interview with Richard Rorty," *Times Literary Supplement*, 24 June 1994, 14.
2. Arnold Simoni, *Beyond Repair: The Urgent Need for a New World Organization* (Don Mills, Ont.: Collier-Macmillan Canada, 1972), xiii.
3. Morris Miller, "Global Governance to Address the Crises of Debt, Poverty and Environment," in Canadian Pugwash Group, *World Security: The New Challenge* (Toronto: Science for Peace/Dundurn Press, 1994), 190.

4. Hew Strachan, "How the war was waged," *Times Literary Supplement*, 5 May 1995, 30.
5. H. Stuart Hughes, *Contemporary Europe: A History* (Englewood Cliffs, N.J., Prentice-Hall, 1961, 1966), 388.
6. Cited in James C. Thomson, "Americans and the 'Loss' of China," in Mark Borthwick, ed., *Pacific Century: The Emergence of Modern Pacific Asia* (Boulder: Westview Press, 1992), 370.
7. Franz Schurmann, *Ideology and Organization in Communist China* (Berkeley and Los Angeles: University of California Press, 1966), xxix.
8. A.J.P. Taylor, *English History 1914–1945* (New York: Oxford University Press, 1965, 1970), 597.
9. Sonia Orwell and Ian Angus, eds., *The Collected Essays, Journalism and Letters of George Orwell* (New York: Harcourt Brace Jovanovich, 1968), 4:180, 309.
10. Ibid., 4:372.
11. Kenneth Boulding, "The Concept of World Interest," in Richard A. Falk and Saul H. Mendlovitz, eds., *The Strategy of World Order* (New York: World Law Fund, 1966), 4:499–500.
12. Alok Rai, *Orwell and the Politics of Despair: A Critical Study of the Writings of George Orwell* (Cambridge: Cambridge University Press, 1988, 1990), x.
13. W.W. Rostow, *The World Economy: History and Prospect* (Austin: University of Texas Press, 1978), 730.
14. For the quoted material here see A.F.W. Plumptre, *Three Decades of Decision: Canada and the World Monetary System, 1944–1975* (Toronto: McClelland and Stewart, 1977), 246–47, 245, 243.
15. John Lukacs, "The End of the Twentieth Century: Historical Reflections on a Misunderstood Epoch," *Harper's*, January 1993, 51.
16. Robert Storbaugh and Daniel Yergin, eds., *Energy Future: Report of the Energy Project at the Harvard Business School* (New York: Random House, 1979), 20, 22.
17. Ibid., 26.
18. Ibid., 28.
19. J.J. Servan-Schreiber, *The American Challenge*, trans. Ronald Steel (New York: Atheneum, 1967, 1968), 3.
20. Heinz Redwood, *The Pharmaceutical Industry – Trends, Problems and Achievements* (London: Oldwicks Press, 1988), 16.
21. United Nations Conference on Trade and Development, *World Investment Report 1994: Transnational Corporations, Employment and the Workplace* (New York and Geneva: United Nations, July 1994), 15.
22. Miller, "Global Governance," 191.
23. Servan-Schreiber, *The American Challenge*, 251.
24. Beijing Review, *15 Years of Economic Reform in China, 1978–93* (Beijing: New Star Publishers, 1994), 3, 4.
25. "New World Economic Order," *Business Week*, 24 July 1978, 68.
26. United Nations Centre on Transnational Corporations, *Transnational Corporations in World Development: Trends and Prospects* (New York: United Nations, 1988), 261.
27. Orwell and Angus, *The Collected Essays, Journalism and Letters of George Orwell*, 1:397.
28. Earl Fry, "The North American Free Trade Agreement: U.S. and Canadian Perspectives," in Joseph A. McKinney and Rebecca Sharpless, eds., *Implications of a North American Free Trade Region: Multidisciplinary Perspectives* (Ottawa: Carleton University Press, 1992), 27.
29. See Rodney Dobell and Michael Neufeld, eds., *Beyond NAFTA: The Western Hemisphere Interface* (Lantzville, B.C.: oolichan books, 1993), 75.
30. *Business Week*, 17 May 1993, 54.
31. Commission on Global Governance, *Our Global Neighborhood* (Oxford: Oxford University Press, 1995), 10.
32. United Nations Conference on Trade and Development, *World Investment Report 1994*, 87.
33. Ibid., 9, 11.
34. *Business Week*, 13 March 1995, 48.
35. United Nations Conference on Trade and Development, *World Investment Report 1994*, 4.
36. Quoted in Robert J. Dowling, "A Less-Than-Perfect Vision of 2020," *Business Week*, 27 March 1995, 18.
37. United Nations Conference on Trade and Development, *World Investment Report 1994*, 74.
38. "Korea," *Business Week*, 31 July 1995, 57.
39. United Nations Conference on Trade and Development, *World Investment Report 1994*, 129.
40. "Borderless Finance: Fuel for Growth," *Business Week/21st Century Capitalism*, 18

November 1994, 40, 41.
41 United Nations Conference on Trade and Development, *World Investment Report 1994*, 126–29.
42 Tom Nairn, "On the Threshold," *London Review of Books*, 23 March 1995, 9, 11. Mr. Nairn himself, as best I can make out, believes that it is "short-sighted" to become too caught up in such views, and that "'modernisation' itself is only another word for 'for ever' – the ongoing process of industrialisation through which in time far greater human and cultural variety will certainly be produced" (11).
43 Organization for Economic Co-operation and Development, *Technology and the Economy: The Key Relationships* (Paris: OECD, 1992), 213.
44 "Ford – Alex Trotman's Daring Global Strategy," *Business Week*, 3 April 1995, 104. The particular critic whose words are quoted here is U.S. automotive manufacturing consultant James Harbour.
45 "Japan's New Identity," *Business Week*, 10 April 1995, 110.

Chapter 4: The First Political Fallout
1 Franz Neumann, *The Democratic and the Authoritarian State: Essays in Political and Legal Theory*, edited and with a preface by Herbert Marcuse (New York: The Free Press, 1957), 181.
2 Milton and Rose Friedman, *Free to Choose* (New York: Avon Books, 1979, 1980, 1981), 273.
3 Ibid., 272, xv, xvi, xvii. The Friedmans' book was also the basis for a television series broadcast on the U.S. PBS network in 1980 (ix).
4 Ibid., 272, xx.
5 Ibid., 273.
6 Murray Sayle, "Bowing to the inevitable," *Times Literary Supplement*, 28 April–4 May 1989, 445.
7 Robert Neff, "Japan May Be Just Catching Its Breath," *Business Week*, 10 April 1995, 19.
8 Beijing Review, *15 Years of Economic Reform in China, 1978–93* (Beijing: New Star Publishers, 1994), 42.
9 William H. Overholt, *The Rise of China: How Economic Reform Is Creating a New Superpower* (New York: W.W. Norton & Co., 1993), 29.
10 "India Shakes Off Its Shackles: Free-Market Reforms Are Stirring up the Country's Long-Stagnant Economy," *Business Week*, 30 January 1995, 49.
11 United Nations Conference on Trade and Development, *World Investment Report 1994: Transnational Corporations, Employment and the Workplace* (New York and Geneva: United Nations, July 1994), 75.
12 "Socialism: Trials and Errors," *Time*, 13 March 1978, 18.
13 Ibid., 20.
14 Max Weber, "Politics as a Vocation," in H.H. Gerth and C. Wright Mills, eds., *From Max Weber: Essays in Sociology* (New York: Oxford University Press, 1946, 1958, 1972), 78.
15 Robert J. Dowling, "Communism in Turmoil," *Business Week*, 5 June 1989, 37.
16 Milovan Djilas, "The East's 'West,'" *Encounter*, December 1987, 8.
17 Onora O'Neill, "Berlin Diary," *London Review of Books*, 12 July 1990, 21.
18 According to preliminary estimates in the 1994 and 1995 editions of *The World Bank Atlas* (Washington: World Bank), the Russian Federation's GNP (in U.S. dollars) fell from $397,786 million in 1992 to $348,413 million in 1993. Parallel declines were reported in other parts of the former Soviet Union, except for Estonia, the Kyrgyz Republic, Latvia, the Ukraine, and Uzbekistan.
19 Quoted in Bill Javetski and John Pearson, "The World Is Waiting for Bush to Lead," *Business Week*, 5 June 1989, 86.
20 Sonia Orwell and Ian Angus, eds., *The Collected Essays, Journalism and Letters of George Orwell* (New York: Harcourt Brace Jovanovich, 1968), 4:375, 372.
21 H. Stuart Hughes, *Contemporary Europe: A History* (Englewood Cliffs, N.J.: Prentice-Hall, 1961, 1966), 463.
22 George Lichtheim, *Europe in the Twentieth Century* (London: Sphere Books, 1972, 1974), 366. Lichtheim also notes how Winston Churchill had told de Gaulle in 1944: "Here is something you should know: whenever we have to choose between Europe and the open sea, we shall always choose the open sea. Whenever I have to choose between you and Roosevelt, I shall always choose Roosevelt."
23 Ibid., 417.
24 David R. Cameron, "The 1992 Initiative: Causes and Consequences," in Alberta M. Sbragia, ed., *Euro-Politics: Institutions and*

Policymaking in the 'New' European Community (Washington: Brookings Institution, 1992), 39.
25. Ibid., 44, 45.
26. John Lukacs, "On the End of the Twentieth Century: Historical Reflections on a Misunderstood Epoch," *Harper's*, January 1993, 56.
27. Cameron, "The 1992 Initiative," 67.
28. These are the words of an anonymous "senior Downing Street official," quoted in Lawrence Ingrassia, "When Does a Relationship Stop Being Special, Britons Wonder," *Globe and Mail*, 1 April 1995, A11.
29. Tom Nairn, "On the Threshold," *London Review of Books*, 23 March 1995, 11.
30. B. Guy Peters, "Bureaucratic Politics and the Institutions of the European Community," in Sbragia, ed., *Euro-Politics*, 111.
31. Cameron, "The 1992 Initiative," 58.
32. Peter Lange, "The Politics of the Social Dimension" in Sbragia, ed., *Euro-Politics*, 256.
33. Ibid., 230.
34. Orwell and Angus, *The Collected Essays, Journalism and Letters of George Orwell*, 4:371.
35. Ibid., 373, 374.
36. John Pinder, *European Community: The Building of a Union* (Oxford: Oxford University Press, 1991), 180.
37. Stephen Clarkson, "Constitutionalizing the Canadian-American Relationship," in Duncan Cameron and Mel Watkins, eds., *Canada under Free Trade* (Toronto: James Lorimer & Co., 1993), 19.
38. Michael Hart, "A Western Hemisphere Trade Agreement: Policy or Pipe Dream?" in Rod Dobell and Michael Neufeld, eds., *Beyond NAFTA: The Western Hemisphere Interface* (Lantzville, B.C.: oolichan books, 1993), 126, 127.
39. Rubens Ricupero in ibid., 68.
40. Maurice Walsh, "The First Crisis of the 21st Century," *London Review of Books*, 23 March 1995, 25.
41. *Toronto Star*, 24 May 1994, C4.
42. Mark Borthwick, *Pacific Century: The Emergence of Modern Pacific Asia* (Boulder: Westview Press, 1992), 522, 515.
43. "Japan's New Identity," *Business Week*, 10 April 1995, 112.
44. United Nations Conference on Trade and Development, *World Investment Report 1994*, 79.
45. Quoted in "Japan's New Identity," 114.
46. Ibid., 110, 111.
47. "A U.S.-Europe Trade Pact? Why Not?" *Business Week*, 8 May 1995, 122.
48. Jock A. Finlayson and Ann Weston, *The GATT, Middle Powers and the Uruguay Round*, Middle Powers in the International System series, no. 5 (Ottawa: North-South Institute, June 1990), 11.
49. Ibid., 13.
50. Ibid., 26.
51. "Send in the Next Batch of Trade Honchos, Please," *Business Week*, 20 March 1995, 31.
52. "Who's Afraid of the World Trade Organization?" *Business Week*, 5 June 1995, 35.
53. Christopher Farrell, "Sir Jimmy Goldsmith Goes Jousting at GATT," *Business Week*, 5 December 1994, 36.
54. Douglas Harbrecht, "GATT: Tales from the Dark Side," *Business Week*, 19 December 1994, 52.

Chapter 5: Cultural Fallout

1. Marshall McLuhan, *The Gutenberg Galaxy* (New York: Signet Books, 1962, 1969), 43.
2. Commission on Global Governance, *Our Global Neighborhood* (Oxford: Oxford University Press, 1995), 7.
3. William Leiss, *Under Technology's Thumb* (Montreal and Kingston: McGill-Queen's University Press, 1990), 5.
4. Organization for Economic Co-operation and Development, *Technology and the Economy: The Key Relationships* (Paris: OECD, 1992), 233.
5. Sonia Orwell and Ian Angus, eds., *The Collected Essays, Journalism and Letters of George Orwell* (New York: Harcourt Brace Jovanovich, 1968), 4:502.
6. "The Passing of 'the Shell Man,'" *Business Week*, 24 April 1995, 134P.
7. Commission on Global Governance, *Our Global Neighborhood*, 206.
8. Joyce Barnathan, "'You Put Your Fate in God's Hands,'" *Business Week*, 24 April 1995, 30A.
9. United Nations Conference on Trade and Development, *World Investment Report 1994: Transnational Corporations, Employment and the Workplace* (New York and Geneva: United Nations, July 1994), 120. In this connection the UN authors themselves cite Arthur Lewis, *Growth and Fluctuations, 1870–1913* (London: Allen and Unwin,

1978); and Imre Firenczi, *International Migration* (New York: National Bureau of Economic Research, 1929).
10. Robert W. Gardiner and Leon F. Bouvier, "The United States," in William J. Serow et al., eds., *Handbook on International Migration* (New York: Greenwood Press, 1990), 348.
11. Ronald F. Moore, "Australia" in ibid., 17. The data reported here are for 1986–87.
12. *Canada Year Book 1992* (Ottawa: Statistics Canada, 1991), 91–93. The data reported here are for 1989.
13. John Salt and Rueben Ford, "The United Kingdom," in Serow et al., eds., *Handbook on International Migration*, 333.
14. Commission on Global Governance, *Our Global Neighborhood*, 206.
15. Robert J. Dowling, "A Less-Than-Perfect Vision of 2020," *Business Week*, 27 March 1995, 18. As spelled out in the notes to the prologue of this book, Cyrus Freidheim's pronouncements appear in Debra Fleenor, "The Coming and Going of the Global Corporation," *Columbia Journal of World Business*, Winter 1993. For Christopher Farrell's contributions, see "The Triple Revolution," *Business Week/21st Century Capitalism*, 18 November 1994.
16. Edward Said, *Culture and Imperialism* (New York: Vintage Books, 1993, 1994), 336.
17. Monica Boyd and Chris Taylor, "Canada," in Serow et al., eds., *Handbook on International Migration*, 37.
18. Farrell, "The Triple Revolution," 23.
19. These numbers draw on various published and unpublished Statistics Canada data, reported more fully in Randall White and David Montgomery, *Who Are We? Changing Patterns of Cultural Diversity on the North Shore of Lake Ontario* (Toronto: Waterfront Regeneration Trust, July 1994).
20. Said, *Culture and Imperialism*, xxvi.
21. Quoted in Ian Buruma, "Behind the Garden Wall," *Times Literary Supplement*, 28 April–4 May 1989, 454.
22. "A U.S.-Europe Trade Pact? Why Not?" *Business Week*, 8 May 1995, 122.
23. Harold Innis, *The Fur Trade in Canada* (Toronto: University of Toronto Press, 1930, 1956, 1970), 383.
24. This, it seems to me, is the not quite articulated assumption that underlies such recent contributions to various branches of North American academic literature as Richard White's *The Middle Ground: Indians, Empires, and Republics in the Great Lakes Region, 1650–1815* (Cambridge: Cambridge University Press, 1991, 1993).
25. Greg Burns, "All the World's a McStage," *Business Week*, 8 May 1995, 8.
26. Carol Goar, "U.S. hopeful snipes at multiculturalism," *Toronto Star*, 9 May 1995, A4.
27. Beth Hawkins, "Oklahoma – A Frightening Glimpse into the Militia Mind," *Now Magazine*, 27 April–3 May 1995, 12.
28. Farrell, "The Triple Revolution," 25.
29. Leiss, *Under Technology's Thumb*, x.
30. Dowling, "A Less-Than-Perfect Vision of 2020," 18.
31. Mark Ridley, "The Microbe's Opportunity," *Times Literary Supplement*, 13 January 1995, 7.
32. John Dwyer, "Why the Germs Are Winning," *Times Literary Supplement*, 13 January 1995, 7.
33. Peter Ackroyd, *T.S. Eliot: A Life* (New York: Simon and Schuster, 1984), 335.
34. T.S. Eliot, *Notes towards the Definition of Culture* (London: Faber and Faber, 1948, 1962), 120–21.

Chapter 6: Tilting at Windmills

1. In an address to the U.S. Senate, 22 January 1917.
2. Commission on Global Governance, *Our Global Neighborhood* (Oxford: Oxford University Press, 1995), xix.
3. Christopher Farrell, "The Triple Revolution," in *Business Week/21st Century Capitalism*, 18 November 1994, 25.
4. Commission on Global Governance, *Our Global Neighborhood*, xix.
5. Sonia Orwell and Ian Angus, eds., *The Collected Essays, Journalism and Letters of George Orwell* (New York: Harcourt Brace Jovanovich, 1968), 4:371.
6. Commission on Global Governance, *Our Global Neighborhood*, 341.
7. Timothy Garton Ash, "Catching the Wrong Bus? Europe's Future and the Great Gamble of Monetary Union," *Times Literary Supplement*, 5 May 1995, 4.
8. John C. Polanyi, "From Peacekeeping to Peace Making," in Eric Fawcett and Hanna Newcombe, eds., *United Nations Reform: Looking Ahead after Fifty Years* (Toronto: Science for Peace/Dundurn Press, 1995), 124.

9 Ibid., 123.
10 Commission on Global Governance, *Our Global Neighborhood*, 10–11.
11 Ibid., 347.
12 Paul R. Erlich and Anne H. Erlich, *Population, Resources, Environment: Issues in Human Ecology* (San Francisco: W.H. Freeman and Co., 1970, 1972), 1, 3, 4.
13 Robert O. Matthews, "On Reforming the Global Environment Facility" in Fawcett and Newcombe, eds., *United Nations Reform*, 218.
14 From Woodrow Wilson, *Constitutional Government in the United States* (1908), cited in *Times Literary Supplement*, 21 May 1993, 3.
15 In this and the following few paragraphs I am drawing on the useful summary in Clive Archer, *International Organizations*, 2d ed. (London and New York: Routledge, 1992), 3–33.
16 H. Stuart Hughes, *Contemporary Europe: A History* (Englewood Cliffs: Prentice-Hall, 1961, 1966), 153.
17 Ibid.
18 Ibid., 453. The "primary responsibility for the maintenance of international peace" is taken from article 24 of the UN Charter.
19 Archer, *International Organizations*, 4.
20 United Nations Conference on Trade and Development, *World Investment Report 1994: Transnational Corporations, Employment and the Workplace* (New York and Geneva: United Nations, July 1994), 122, 126.
21 Archer, *International Organizations*, 18.
22 Charles L. Mee Jr., *The End of Order: Versailles 1919* (New York: E.P Dutton, 1980), 262–263.
23 "No Free Ride for Free Trade," *Business Week*, 22 May 1995, 124.
24 Max Weber, "Politics as a Vocation," in H.H. Gerth and C. Wright Mills, eds., *From Max Weber: Essays in Sociology* (New York: Oxford University Press, 1946, 1958, 1972), 78.
25 Archer, *International Organizations*, 16.
26 Hannah Arendt, *Men in Dark Times* (New York: Harcourt, Brace & World, 1968), 81. The passage is from an essay first published in 1957.
27 Commission on Global Governance, *Our Global Neighborhood*, xvi.
28 Arnold Simoni, "A United Nations Peace Force," in Fawcett and Newcombe, *United Nations Reform*, 155.
29 Commission on Global Governance, *Our Global Neighborhood*, 340.
30 Douglas Roche, "The United Nations of the Future," in Fawcett and Newcombe, *United Nations Reform*, 319.
31 Commission on Global Governance, *Our Global Neighborhood*, 338.
32 Simoni, "A United Nations Peace Force," 156.
33 Canadian Committee for the Fiftieth Anniversary of the United Nations, "Canadian Priorities for United Nations Reform," in Fawcett and Newcombe, *United Nations Reform*, 309.
34 Science for Peace Workshop on United Nations Reform, "Recommendations to the Commission on Global Governance," in Fawcett and Newcombe, *United Nations Reform*, 303.
35 Commission on Global Governance, *Our Global Neighbourhood*, 344.
36 Ibid., 148.
37 Morris Miller, "Global Governance to Address the Crises of Debt, Poverty and Environment," in Carl G. Jacobsen et al., eds., *World Security: The New Challenge* (Toronto: Science for Peace/Dundurn Press, 1994), 191.
38 "Mr. Mulroney and the challenge of China," *Globe and Mail*, 15 April 1995, D6.
39 "World Trade: Will China Agree to Pay Its Dues?" *Business Week*, 26 December 1994, 86.
40 Thomas L. Friedman, "Sorry, but this Group of Seven doesn't make the grade," *Globe and Mail*, 30 May 1995, A17.
41 Commission on Global Governance, *Our Global Neighborhood*, 219.
42 R.T. Naylor, *Hot Money and the Politics of Debt* (Montreal: Black Rose Books, 1987, 1994), 328.
43 Dean Foust, "What the IMF Needs Is a Good Alarm System," *Business Week*, 20 February 1995, 55.
44 An example is Miller, "Global Governance."
45 Commission on Global Governance, *Our Global Neighborhood*, 342, 344.
46 Cited in Miller, "Global Governance," 200.
47 "From All-for-One to Free-for-All," *Business Week*, 8 May 1995, 35. Some collective action to stabilize the value of the U.S. dollar, by the U.S. and eleven other countries, had nonetheless begun by the end of May.
48 "Your Move, Japan," *Business Week*, 22 May 1995, 40.
49 "Send in the Next Batch of Trade Honchos, Please," *Business Week*, 20 March 1995, 31.

50 Commission on Global Governance, *Our Global Neighborhood*, 32, 34.
51 Graeme MacQueen, ed., *Unarmed Forces: Nonviolent Action in Central America and the Middle East* (Toronto: Science for Peace/Samuel Stevens, 1992).
52 Saul Alinsky, *Rules for Radicals* (New York: Vintage Books, 1971).

Chapter 7: The Fate of the National State

1 Quoted in Nanette Byrnes, "Up on Down Markets," *Business Week*, 27 February 1995, 101. Brandes is president of Brandes Investment Partners in Del Mar, Calif.: "Over the past 10 years" his "international equity portfolio" has shown "a tidy annual return of 23%."
2 See, for example, Mathew Horsman and Andrew Marshall, *After the Nation-State: Citizens, Tribalism and the New World Disorder* (London: HarperCollins Publishers, 1994); and David J. Elkins, *Beyond Sovereignty: Territory and Political Economy in the Twenty-First Century* (Toronto: University of Toronto Press, 1995).
3 Franz Neumann, *The Democratic and the Authoritarian State: Essays in Political and Legal Theory*, edited and with a preface by Herbert Marcuse (New York: The Free Press, 1957), 168, 181–82.
4 Ibid., 268.
5 D. Mackenzie Brown, *The White Umbrella: Indian Political Thought from Manu to Ghandi* (Berkeley: University of California Press, 1964), 14.
6 Neumann, *The Democratic and the Authoritarian State*, 8.
7 Sonia Orwell and Ian Angus, eds., *The Collected Essays, Journalism and Letters of George Orwell* (New York: Harcourt Brace Jovanovich, 1968), 4:463.
8 Commission on Global Governance, *Our Global Neighborhood* (Oxford: Oxford University Press, 1995), 11.
9 United Nations Conference on Trade and Development, *World Investment Report 1994: Transnational Corporations, Employment and the Workplace* (New York and Geneva: United Nations, July 1994), 119.
10 Nancy Ettlinger, "The Localization of Development in Comparative Perspective," *Economic Geography* 70, no. 2 (April 1994): 144, 147.
11 You can see all this at work in Ron Chernow's discussion of the Morgan banker Thomas Lamont and Mexico's debt troubles in the 1920s and 1930s, in *The House of Morgan: An American Banking Dynasty and the Rise of Modern Finance* (New York: Simon & Schuster, 1990), 237–43, 296–99.
12 Edward Greenspon, "PM Urges Monetary Sovereignty," *Globe and Mail*, 15 May 1995, A4.
13 Quoted in R.T. Naylor, *Hot Money and the Politics of Debt* (Montreal: Black Rose Books, 1987, 1994), 12.
14 "Borderless Finance: Fuel for Growth," *Business Week/21st Century Capitalism*, 18 November 1994, 41.
15 Quoted in ibid., 41.
16 Earl Fry, "The North American Free Trade Agreement: U.S. and Canadian Perspectives," in Joseph A. McKinney and Rebecca Sharpless, eds., *Implications of a North American Free Trade Region: Multidisciplinary Perspectives* (Ottawa: Carleton University Press, 1992), 26. The survey was conducted by the Institute for Social Research, University of Michigan.
17 Robert Neff, "Why Japanese Deregulation Won't Much Help America," *Business Week*, 3 April 1995, 72.
18 United Nations Conference on Trade and Development, *World Investment Report 1994*, 72–76.
19 David S. Landes, *The Unbound Prometheus: Technological Change and Industrial Development in Western Europe from 1750 to the Present* (Cambridge: Cambridge University Press, 1969), 7.
20 Orwell and Angus, *The Collected Essays, Journalism and Letters of George Orwell*, 4:411.
21 Ibid., 4:427–428.
22 See Orwell's views on "the main functions of the State" (which include "to protect" the "newborn citizen ... against economic exploitation by individuals or groups") in Bernard Crick, *Orwell: A Life* (Boston: Little, Brown and Co., 1980), 344–45.
23 This postwar minimalist notion of democracy as a "political method" owes a great deal to Joseph Schumpeter, *Capitalism, Socialism and Democracy* (New York: Harper & Row, 1942, 1947, 1950, 1975), chaps. 12 and 13. There has subsequently been a quite vast academic literature.

24 Cited in A.F.W. Plumptre, *Three Decades of Decision: Canada and the World Monetary System, 1944–1975* (Toronto: McClelland and Stewart, 1977), 53.
25 John Lukacs, *Outgrowing Democracy: A History of the United States in the Twentieth Century* (New York: Doubleday & Co., 1984).
26 "Mr. Mulroney and the Challenge of China," *Globe and Mail*, 15 April 1995, D6.
27 Dr. Kenneth Courtis, vice-president, Deutsche Bank Capital Markets, in Rodney Dobell and Michael Neufeld, eds., *Beyond NAFTA: The Western Hemisphere Interface* (Lantzville, B.C.: oolichan books, 1993), 34.
28 John Templeman, "When Will Germany Stop Sleepwalking?", *Business Week*, 29 May 1995, 48.
29 "Behind the Fed's Not-to-Worry Stance," *Business Week*, 17 April 1995, 35.
30 Tom Nairn, "On the Threshold," *London Review of Books*, 23 March 1995, 9.
31 *Basic Facts About The United Nations* (New York: United Nations, Department of Public Information, 1992, 1994), 265.
32 Timothy Garton Ash, "Catching the Wrong Bus?: Europe's Future and the Great Gamble of Monetary Union," *Times Literary Supplement*, 5 May 1995, 3.
33 Geoffrey Barraclough, ed., *The Times Atlas of World History* (London: Times Books, 1978), 144–45.
34 Neumann, *The Democratic and the Authoritarian State*, 181.
35 Orwell and Angus, *The Collected Essays, Journalism and Letters of George Orwell*, 3:362.
36 Ibid., 3:363.
37 Nairn, "On the Threshold," 10. Nairn also talks about the "state nation" in this context – a concept broadly comparable, it would seem, to what I have called the "national state" in this book.
38 See, for example, the discussion on the large-scale "adoption" of Huron into Iroquois societies, following the mid-seventeenth-century Iroquois conquest of the Huron confederacy in the Great Lakes region, in Bruce G. Trigger, *The Children of Aataentsic II: A History of the Huron People to 1660* (Montreal and Kingston: McGill-Queen's University Press, 1976), 826–31.

Epilogue
1 I heard Henry Kissinger say something of this sort about the problems of managing world issues, on a U.S. public affairs television show (probably the "McNeil-Lehrer News Hour"). I have estimated the exact year as 1984, as a final homage to George Orwell – who thought about many of the same kinds of things as Henry Kissinger, from a different point of view.
2 John Bowle, *The Imperial Achievement: The Rise and Transformation of the British Empire* (Harmondsworth: Penguin Books, 1974, 1977), 556.
3 United Nations Conference on Trade and Development, *World Investment Report 1994: Transnational Corporations, Employment and the Workplace* (New York and Geneva: United Nations, July 1994), 135.
4 James Gillies, "Henry Mintzberg – Strategically Speaking," *acumen*, May/June 1995, 24.
5 Thomas L. Friedman, "Sorry, but This Group of Seven Doesn't Make the Grade," *Globe and Mail*, 30 May 1995, A17. The quoted passage is conveying the views of Jeffrey Garten, U.S. under-secretary of commerce for international trade. The item first appeared in the *New York Times*.
6 Edward W. Said, *Culture and Imperialism* (New York: Vintage Books, 1993, 1994), 5.
7 Bowle, *The Imperial Achievement*, 554.
8 Sonia Orwell and Ian Angus, eds., *The Collected Essays, Journalism and Letters of George Orwell* (New York: Harcourt Brace Jovanovich, 1968), 4:374.
9 Franz Neumann, *The Democratic and the Authoritarian State: Essays in Political and Legal Theory*, edited and with a preface by Herbert Marcuse (New York: The Free Press, 1957), 182–83.
10 Daphne Patai, *The Orwell Mystique: A Study in Male Ideology* (Amherst: University of Massachusetts Press, 1984). And see John Rodden, *The Politics of Literary Reputation: The Making and Claiming of 'St. George' Orwell* (New York: Oxford University Press, 1989).
11 Harold Innis, *The Bias of Communication* (Toronto: University of Toronto Press, 1951, 1971), 61.
12 Alan Ryan, "The Middling Sort," *London Review of Books*, 25 May 1995, 13.

INDEX

Achebe, Chinua, 84
Afghanistan, 92
African influence on American culture, 18, 84
Agriculture, 15, 31, 49, 94
AIDS, 87
Air travel, 37, 75, 77, 79
Alcan Aluminum, 41
Alcatel Alsthom, 39, 41
Algeria, 9, 13, 45, 47
Alternative model of industrialization, 35, 40, 42, 43, 49, 61-62
American Civil War, 22, 80
American War of Independence, 20, 21, 32
Amoco, 41
Andorra, 120
Anglo-Egyptian Sudan, 25
Antibiotics, 87
Apache, 22, 84
Arabic numerals, 31-32
Arendt, Hannah, 97, 98, 113
Argentina, 9, 13, 14, 18, 67, 92, 104
Arkwright, Richard, 32
Armenia, 120
Asea Brown Boveri, 41
ASEAN Free Trade Area (AFTA), 68-70, 99, 117
Ash, Timothy Garton, 65, 92
Asia-Pacific Economic Co-operation forum (APEC), 68-70
Asian tigers, 51, 54
Asiatic influence on Greek culture, 31
Association of South-East Asian Nations (ASEAN), 68-70
Astrolabe, 31, 76
Atlee, Clement, 43
Atomic bomb, 91
Atomic power, 37
Australia, 14, 18, 21, 26, 68, 70, 79, 80- 84, 88, 104
Austria, 14, 19, 64, 80
Automation, 36, 53
Automobile industry, 33, 38, 39, 54, 114, 123
Ayatollah Khomeni, 86
Azerbaijan, 120

B.A.T. Industries, 41
Bacon, Francis, 32
Bagehot, Walter, 3
Baker, James A., 63
Bangladesh, 2, 13
Barings PLC merchant bank, 54, 77
Barricades scenario, 73, 106, 125
BASF, 41
Battle of Mukden, 23
Bayer, 39, 41
BBC World News, 84
Belarus, 63
Belgian Congo, 45
Belgium, 14, 24, 25, 39, 41, 64, 65, 104, 105
Berlin wall, 6, 62, 71
Biodiversity, 94
Biotechnology, 86-87
Blair, Tony, 65
Blinder, Alan, 115
BMW, 41
Bosnia and Hercegovina, 120
Boulding, Kenneth, 43-44

Bourgeoisie, 2, 4, 20, 27, 34, 35, 40, 58, 88, 90, 105, 112, 126
Bourgeois, Léon, 96-97
Boutros-Ghali, Boutros, 98
Bowle, John, 122, 124
Brandes, Charles H., 105
Brazil, 13, 14, 16-18, 51- 53, 63, 67, 80, 99, 100, 104, 119
Bretton Woods system, 46, 48, 54, 55, 58, 69, 94, 99-102, 108
Bridgestone, 41
British empire, 17, 19-21, 23, 25, 29, 43, 45, 59, 69, 84, 124, 125
British Petroleum, 41
Brunei, 69, 79
Buchanan, Patrick, 85
Buddhism, 34
Bulgaria, 43

Canada, 9, 13, 14, 20, 21, 41, 49, 63, 67, 68, 70, 79-84, 88, 89, 100, 104, 112, 117, 119, 123, 125
Canada-U.S. trade agreement, 67
Capitalism, 4, 8, 11, 24, 34, 35, 40, 43-45, 56, 78, 112, 122, 127
Caribbean countries, 52, 66, 81, 115
Carter, Jimmy, 59, 91
Charter of Fundamental Social Rights, 65
Chaucer, Geoffrey, 31
Chemical industries, 33
Cherokee, 22, 84
Chevron, 41
Chile, 52, 67
China, 4, 8, 13, 14, 16, 17, 19, 20, 23, 24, 28, 31, 34, 40, 42, 43, 49, 50-53, 57, 60, 62- 64, 69-72, 76, 80-83, 95, 98-100, 103, 104, 110, 113, 116, 128
Chinese imperial expansion, 19
Chinese Revolution, 43
Chrétien, Jean, 68
Christianity, 1, 15, 19, 23, 31, 107
Chrysler, 41
Ciba-Geigy, 41
Civic nation, 118-19
Civil Rights movement in the U.S., 75
Clinton, Bill, 7, 53, 59, 67, 72
Club of Rome, 35
CNN World News, 84
Cold War, 11, 44, 48, 61-63, 65, 71, 92, 95, 98, 103, 127
Colombia, 13
Columbus, Christopher, 17, 122
Colonial governance structures, 24, 25, 96
Commission on Global Governance, 91, 93, 97-99, 101, 103, 107
Communism, 1, 7, 40, 43, 44, 49, 62, 78, 126
Competition, 4, 9, 63, 67, 86, 106, 111, 114
Computer technology, 37, 75
Confucius, 4, 60, 86
Cree, 84
Croatia, 120
Cuban missile crisis, 91
Culbert, S., 28
Cultural backlash, 11, 85-88, 128
Cultural diversity, 8, 80-85, 89, 117-19, 124-27

Culture wars, 4, 26, 86
Currency issues, 46, 52, 68, 69, 100-2, 112
Czech Republic, 120
Czechoslovakia, 43

da Gama, Vasco, 16
Daimler Benz, 41
de Gaulle, Charles, 64
de Tocqueville, Alexis, 20, 126
Decolonization, 25-27, 44-45, 66, 75, 96, 110
Defaulting on debt, 22, 101
Democracy, 4, 11, 35, 40, 44, 45, 85, 97, 103, 105, 106, 112-15, 119, 126
Denmark, 14, 64, 65
Design of computer chips and software in India, 32, 124
Developing countries, 38-40, 42, 44, 45, 50-53, 58, 68, 71, 72, 101, 102, 109-11, 123
Diaz, Bartholomew, 16, 87, 122, 126
Djilas, Milovan, 62
Dow Chemical, 41
Dowling, Robert J., 81-82
Drug trade, 20, 93
Du Pont, 41
Dutch empire, 23, 44-45
Dyarchy in British India, 25

East India Company (British), 19, 39
East India Company (Dutch), 39
Eastman Kodak, 41
Economic Security Council proposal, 101
Ecuador, 47
Edison, Thomas, 33
Education, 4, 25, 79, 107, 112
Egypt, 13, 25, 47, 116
Electrical industries, 33, 38
Electrolux, 41
Electronics industries, 53
Elf Aquitaine, 41
Eliot, T.S., 87-88, 107
Energy issues, 36, 42, 46, 47, 50, 52, 55, 58, 64
Enforced liberalism of the colonial era, 96
ENI, 41
Environmental issues, 4, 35, 36, 38, 93-94, 99, 101, 102
Equality, 31, 34-36, 110, 111, 116
Eritrea, 120
Estonia, 63, 120
Ethiopia, 13, 25, 95
Ethnic cleansing, 82
Ettlinger, Nancy, 108
Eurointellectuals, 65
European Coal and Steel Community, 64
European Economic Community, 64
European integration, 63-66, 71
European Union, 65-68, 71, 83, 99, 105, 110, 115-17
Exxon, 39, 41

Fascism, 78
Falkland Islands, 92
Farrell, Christopher, 1-8, 10, 15, 24, 40, 58, 63, 73, 79, 81-83, 85, 86, 90, 105, 112, 121, 124
Fiat, 41
Financial industry, 40, 54, 100, 101
Finland, 14, 64
First industrial revolution, 29-32, 34-36, 38, 45, 46, 53, 86, 93, 110

First manned space ship, 61
First people on the moon, 122
First World War, 19, 24, 25, 39, 46, 90-92, 95, 122
Fleenor, Debra, 3
Ford Motor Company, 39, 41, 55, 78, 123, 124
Ford, Henry, 33, 60
Foreign direct investment, 24, 45, 48, 50-52, 55, 60-61, 108
France, 7, 13, 14, 16-20, 39, 41, 44, 48, 49, 53, 57, 64, 67, 80, 81, 83-86, 88, 92, 95, 96, 104, 115, 116
Free Trade Agreement of the Americas proposal, 67
Free-market reform, 11, 49, 51, 52, 58-63, 65, 71, 72, 82, 106, 110, 122
Freidheim, Cyrus, 3, 6, 55, 81, 82, 123
French empire, 23, 25, 45
French Revolution, 20, 128
Fry, Earl, 51
Fuji Xerox Company, 56
Fukuyama, Francis, 7

Gabon, 47
Garten, Jeffrey, 100
Gender issues, 3, 79, 107, 127
Gene management, 86-87
General Agreement on Tariffs and Trade (GATT), 11, 66, 70-74, 94, 99, 106, 108, 115
General Electric, 39, 41
General Motors, 39, 41
Geographic dispersal of industrial production, 38, 50, 111
Georgia, 63, 120
Germany, 13, 14, 19, 24, 25, 39, 41, 42, 43, 48, 49, 57, 62, 64, 65, 69, 80, 83, 88, 95, 100, 102, 104, 106, 108, 114-18
Ghana, 45
Glaxo Holdings, 41
Global corporation, 3, 6, 40, 54-56, 81, 123
Global economic development strategy, 109, 110, 112
Global economic integration, 54-56, 78, 122-123
Global Environment Facility, 94
Global middle class, 1, 7, 81-82, 88, 124, 126
Global warming, 94
Globalization of culture, 8, 81-85, 127
Godfrey, John, 115
Gold (in Bretton Woods system), 46
Goldsmith, James, 73
Gorbachev, Mikhail, 61, 62
Government expenditure as a share of GNP, 44, 61
Grand Metropolitan, 41
Great Depression, 39
Greater East Asia Co-Prosperity Sphere, 68
Greece, 14, 31, 64, 83
Greenpeace, 123
Gross national product (purchasing power parity), 63, 99, 100, 104
Gross national product (standard measure), 9, 14, 63, 100, 104
Group of Seven, 48-49, 94, 100-2

Hague conferences, 93-96
Haiti, 51
Hanseatic League, 117
Hanson, 41
Harmonization, 108
Hawke, Bob, 70
Health companies, 2
Hegel, G.W.F., 7

High imperial globalization era (1870-1913), 23, 24, 39, 80, 90, 95, 110, 112, 122
Hinduism, 4, 86
Hitachi, 39, 41
Hitler, Adolf, 77
Hobsbawm, Eric, 38-39, 45
Hoechst, 41
Holderbank, 41
Homophobia, 127
Honda, 41
Hong Kong, 14, 21, 28, 42, 51, 53, 57, 70, 79, 81
House of Morgan, 22
Human origins, 15
Human rights, 1, 81
Hungary, 43, 80, 83
Huntington, Samuel P., 4, 27
Hussein, Saddam, 26

IBM, 39, 41
ICI, 41
Identity politics, 26
Ideology, 6-8, 11, 82, 88, 99, 111, 114, 118, 123-28
Ieyasu, Tokugawa, 23
Ilsley, J.L., 112
Imperialism, 10, 15-27, 30, 36, 39, 44, 51, 63-64, 72, 82, 84, 96, 118, 122, 124-27
India, 8, 13, 14, 16, 17, 19, 21, 24-26, 28, 31, 32, 40, 44, 45, 52, 53, 57, 60-61, 63, 64, 69, 80, 83, 89, 99, 100, 104, 116, 119, 124
Indian National Congress, 25, 44
Indonesia, 2, 13, 14, 17, 21, 24, 28, 44, 45, 47, 51, 69, 80, 110
Inflation, 54, 59, 109
Information Revolution, 1, 2, 37, 38, 50, 54, 75-79, 107, 108, 113
Innis, Harold, 34
Intelsat telephone circuit, 37
International division of labour, 53-54
International financial system, 8, 9, 22, 45-46, 50, 52, 54, 94, 101, 107-9
International Monetary Fund, 46, 70, 94, 101, 112
International Trade Organization proposal, 70-71
Internationale, 7
Iran, 13, 14, 47, 59
Iraq, 47
Ireland, 64
Iron and steel industry, 33, 61
Iroquois, 84
Islam, 4, 31, 34, 69, 86
Israel, 116
Itachu Corporation, 41
Italy, 13, 14, 24, 25, 41, 44, 49, 64, 72, 79, 80, 83, 95, 104, 108, 115
ITT, 41

Jacobs, Jane, 9
Jamaica, 57
Japan, 10, 13, 14, 16, 17, 19, 23, 26, 30, 33, 40-45, 48, 49-57, 59, 60, 66-70, 72, 77, 79, 83, 95, 100, 102, 104, 114, 115
Japanese imperialism, 48, 68-69
Johnson, Chalmers, 60
Jordan, 116
Jungnickel, R., 57

Kanji, Nishio, 83
Kassler, Peter, 73

Kazakhstan, 120
Kissinger, Henry, 101, 121
Korea, 23, 45
Korean War, 45
Krugman, Paul, 53
Kuwait, 47
Kyrgyz Republic, 63, 120

La Francophonie, 125
Labour and wages, 4, 7, 34, 35, 50, 51, 53, 54, 57, 63, 68, 83, 108, 114
Languages, 18, 28, 59, 78, 80, 83-85, 88, 116, 121, 123, 125, 126, 127
Latin American independence movements, 20, 22
Latvia, 120
Le Pen, Jean-Marie, 85
League of Nations, 91, 92, 95, 96, 103
Lebanon, 81
Leiss, William, 86
Lenin, Vladimir Ilyich, 24, 62
Letterman, David, 124
Lever Brothers, 39
Liberia, 25
Libya, 47
Liechtenstein, 116, 117, 120
Liemt, G. van, 57
Limits to industrial growth, 35
Lithuania, 120
Lomé Convention, 66, 115
Lovell, Jeremy, 116
Luddites, 35, 86, 93
Lukacs, John, 113
Luxembourg, 64, 105
Lyonnaise des Eaux, 41

Maastricht, 64
Macedonia, 120
Magellan, Ferdinand, 17
Malaysia, 28, 45, 52, 53, 57, 69, 70, 80, 81, 83, 110, 117, 125
Malta, 21
Manchester School, 106
Manchuko, 23
Mandela, Nelson, 75
Manufacturing, 24, 33, 51, 53, 60, 62
Mao Zedong, 42, 43, 49, 64
Marshall Islands, 120
Marubeni, 41
Marx, Karl, 7, 22, 34, 35, 62, 73, 122, 128
Matsushita Electric, 39, 41
Maxwell, James Clerk, 33
Maya, 84
McCarthy witch-hunt, 44
McDonald's, 84
McLaren, Roy, 68
McLuhan, Marshall, 75, 76, 82
Medicine, 38, 86-87
Meijer, Ron, 6
Meiji Restoration, 23
Mercantilism, 60, 70
MERCOSUR trade pact, 67, 70, 99, 117
Mexico, 13, 14, 16, 18, 22, 52, 57, 67, 68, 101, 104, 109
Meyer, John, 1, 81
Michelin, 39, 41
Microelectronics revolution, 10, 37, 39, 54. 108
Micronesia, 119, 120
Middle ground in North America, 84

Migrations, 18, 24, 75, 79-85
Militarism, 48, 127
Ming dynasty, 19
Mintzberg, Henry, 123
Mitsui, 41
Mitterand, Fránçois, 92
Mobil, 41
Moldova, 120
Monaco, 120
Monroe Doctrine, 22
Morison, Samuel Eliot, 19, 91
Morocco, 57, 72, 116
Motion pictures, 33, 38, 76
Mulroney, Brian, 100
Multinational corporations. *See* Transnational corporations
Muslim League, 44
Myanmar ("Burma"), 13, 21, 24, 44, 45, 80

Naipaul, V.S., 1, 84, 105
Namibia, 120
Napoleonic Wars, 20
Narayan, R.K., 84
Nation-state (national state), 11, 12, 62, 93, 95, 96, 105-20, 126
National modes of production, 108
National Socialism, 126
Nationalism, 118
NEC Corporation, 41
Nestlé, 39, 41
Netherlands, 6, 14, 16-19, 23, 41, 64, 65, 72, 83, 95, 104
Neumann, Franz, 58, 106, 126
Neutron bomb, 91
New Zealand, 18, 21, 68, 70, 79, 81, 83, 84, 88
Newton, Isaac, 32
Nigeria, 2, 13, 47
Nissan Motor, 41
Nissho Iwai, 41
Nixon, Richard, 46
Noda, Nobuo, 69
Non-governmental organizations (NGOs), 91, 102
Non-Proliferation Treaty, 91
Non-tariff barriers, 71, 108
North American Free Trade Agreement (NAFTA), 67-68, 70, 99, 109, 114, 117
North Korea, 120
Norway, 14

O'Brien, Richard, 8
October War, 47
Oklahoma City bombing, 77, 85
Opium War, 20
Organization of Petroleum Exporting Countries (OPEC), 47-48, 50, 58, 64, 110
Origins of mathematics in India 32
Orwell, George, 8, 10, 29, 30, 35, 36, 43, 44, 51, 55, 62, 63, 64, 65, 66, 69, 77, 78, 86, 91,107, 111, 118, 125, 127
Ottoman Turks, 17
Ozone depletion, 94

Pakistan, 13, 28, 44, 53, 81
Paraguay, 67
Partition of Africa, 24, 25
Patai, Daphne, 127-28
Peabody, George, 22
Pechiney, 41

Pepsico, 41
Perry, Matthew, 22
Petrofina, 41
Philip Morris, 41
Philippines, 13, 20, 28, 69, 79, 81, 83
Philips Electronics, 41
Phonograph records, 33, 76
Poland, 13, 14, 43, 81, 83
Political correctness, 8, 26, 82
Pollution of international waters, 94
Population, 6, 9, 13, 16, 86, 94, 116, 120
Populism, 9
Portugal, 14, 16-20, 23, 31, 37, 64, 83, 86
Portuguese empire, 16-20, 25, 76
Pottier, Eugène, 7
Printing and moveable type, 34, 76
Proctor & Gamble, 41
Proletariat, 7, 30, 35, 126

Qatar, 47
Qing (Manchu) dynasty, 19
Quebec, 9, 117

Radio, 33, 76, 88
Railways, 33
Rapoport, Anatol and Anthony, 95
Re-Asianization, 56, 68-69
Reagan, Ronald, 8, 59, 91, 92
Regional trade agreements, 11, 66-70, 108, 117
Reich, Robert, 7, 8
Renaissance in Europe, 34
Renault, 41
Resource industries, 24
Rhône-Poulenc, 41
Ricupero, Rubens, 51
Rio Conference on Environment and Development, 102
Robert Bosch, 41
Roche Holdings, 41
Role of science in technological development, 33
Roman empire, 16, 21
Roman numerals, 32
Rorty, Richard, 42
Royal Dutch Shell, 39, 41, 73, 78, 106, 125
RTZ, 41
Ruggerio, Renato, 72, 100
Rule of law, 90, 93
Rumania, 43
Russian empire, 21-23, 63, 95
Russian Federation, 13, 14, 62-63, 69, 71, 72, 99, 100, 104
Russian Revolution, 22, 39, 43

Said, Edward, 26, 30, 82-85, 124, 125
Saint Gobain, 41
San Marino, 120
Sandoz, 41
Saudi Arabia, 14, 47, 79
Schuman, Robert, 64
Schumpeter, Joseph, 4
Scientific breakthroughs (1859-74), 33
Seagram, 41
Second industrial revolution, 33, 36, 38, 46
Second World War, 8, 10, 23, 40, 42, 46, 48, 55, 56, 61, 63, 64, 87, 91, 92, 95-97, 102, 110, 112, 118, 119, 122, 128
Secretary General, 95, 98
Servan-Schreiber, Jean-Jacques, 48, 49

Seven Years' War, 19-21, 91
Sharp, 41
Shrinkage of distance, 37
Siemens, 41
Singapore, 21, 42, 51, 54, 61, 69, 77, 79, 116, 117
Single European Act, 64
Sino-Japanese War, 23
Sioux, 22, 84
Slave trade, 18, 80
Slovakia, 120
Slovenia, 120
Smith, Adam, 20, 59, 60, 61, 66, 67, 72, 90, 94, 99, 105, 106, 119, 124, 128
Social welfare state, 35, 43-45, 65, 110-12, 114
Socialism, 8, 11, 30, 34-36, 40, 43-45, 49, 59-61, 63, 65, 66, 78, 87, 111, 125
Socialist market economy, 60-62
Soil erosion, 36
Solvay, 39, 41
Sony, 41
Soros, George, 109
South Africa, 13, 14, 57, 75, 80, 81
South Korea, 13, 14, 42, 51, 53, 54, 61, 70, 72, 104, 110, 120
Spain, 13, 14, 16-20, 31, 32, 63, 64, 79, 83, 104
Spanish empire, 16-20, 22, 25
Sri Lanka (Ceylon), 17, 28, 44, 45, 80, 81
Stalin, Joseph, 77, 95
Stanford University, 1, 81
Steam engine, 32, 33
Sudan, 13
Sultan Baab, 17
Sultan of Bijapur, 16
Sweden, 14, 19, 41, 64, 104
Switzerland, 14, 39, 41, 71, 74, 80, 95, 104, 116, 117
Syria, 116

Taipan, 2, 5, 6, 15, 128
Taiwan, 23, 51, 61, 70
Tajikistan, 120
Tanzania, 9, 13
Technology, 4, 10, 29-41, 43, 50, 53-56, 58, 60-62, 75-78, 86, 90, 107-11, 119
Telecommunication technologies, 37, 38
Telescreens and Big Brother, 77
Television, 8, 37, 39, 54, 55, 59, 60, 75, 76, 84, 124
Terrorism, 77, 93
Texaco, 41
Textile industry, 32, 33, 38, 53, 54, 57
Thailand, 13, 14, 16, 42, 52, 69, 80
Thatcher, Margaret, 8, 59, 65, 91
Third and fourth industrial revolutions, 36-38, 42, 50, 58, 107, 108, 110
Thirty Years' War, 96
Thomson Corporation, 41
Tito, 43
Tobin, James, 100-101
Tokugawa shogunate, 23, 56, 115
Toshiba, 41
Total, 41
Totalitarianism, 1, 44, 62, 77-78, 103, 106, 115
Tourism, 75, 79
Toyota Motor Co., 41
Trade issues, 55, 66-73, 106-109, 115, 125
Transatlantic Free Trade Agreement proposal (TAFTA), 68, 70
Transnational corporations, 7-9, 26, 38-41, 43, 45-48, 50-53, 58, 60, 61, 63, 69, 73, 78, 81, 84, 85, 101, 107-9, 123
Treaty of Kanagawa, 23
Treaty of Westphalia, 96
"Triad" (Western Europe/North America/Japan), 40, 55, 56
Trotman, Alex, 123, 124
Tuberculosis, 87
Tunisia, 25, 116
Turkey, 13, 14
Turkmenistan, 120

U.S.S.R., 2, 11, 21, 22, 35, 40, 42, 43, 48-50, 61-64, 66, 92, 95, 110, 118, 128
Ukraine, 13, 14, 63, 83
Unilever, 41
United Arab Emirates, 47, 79
United Kingdom, 13, 14, 16-19, 29-33, 39, 41, 43, 44, 46, 49, 54, 55, 57, 59, 64, 65, 74, 78, 79, 81-84, 86-88, 91, 92, 95, 101, 104, 106, 108, 110, 117, 123, 124
United Nations, 5, 8, 11, 23, 24, 39-41, 45, 46, 51, 53, 55, 57, 79, 85, 90-92, 94-98, 102, 103, 113, 116-19, 120, 123
United Nations Peace Force proposals, 97, 98
United States, 2, 4, 7, 9, 13, 14, 20, 22-24, 26, 29, 32, 33, 40-44, 46-53, 55-57, 59-61, 65-72, 75, 80-86, 88, 91-93, 95, 96, 100-102, 104, 106, 108-10, 113-16, 118, 119, 123, 124, 126
Uruguay, 67
Uzbekistan, 63, 120

Veba, 41
Venezuela, 47
Veto in UN Security Council, 95
Vietnam, 2, 13, 45, 46, 53, 69, 81, 83, 92
Vietnam War, 45, 46, 56, 69, 92
Volkswagen, 41
Volvo, 41

Walcott, Derek, 84
Wallerstein, Immanuel, 16
Walpole, Horace, 20
Warner, Marina, 115
Watt, James, 33
Watts, W., 15
Weakness of globalizing trends in Africa, 52, 110
Weakness of neoclassical economics, 60, 61
Western Hemisphere, 18, 67-68, 70, 79
Wilson, Woodrow, 90, 96
World Bank, 13, 14, 46, 63, 70, 94, 100, 104, 119, 120
World car concept, 55
World Trade Centre bombing, 77
World Trade Organization (WTO), 11, 70-73, 94, 100, 102

Xerox, 41

Yugoslavia, 43, 62, 83

Zaire, 13
Zhou Enlai, 128
Zimbabwe, 16

TOWARDS THE NEW MILLENNIUM SERIES

Anthony Westell, *Reinventing Canada,* 1994
David Matas, *No More: The Battle against Human Rights Violations,* 1994
Randall White, *Global Spin: Probing the Globalization Debate,* 1995
Don Waterfall, *Dismantling Leviathan: Cutting Government Down to Size,* 1995